God Leads Us Along

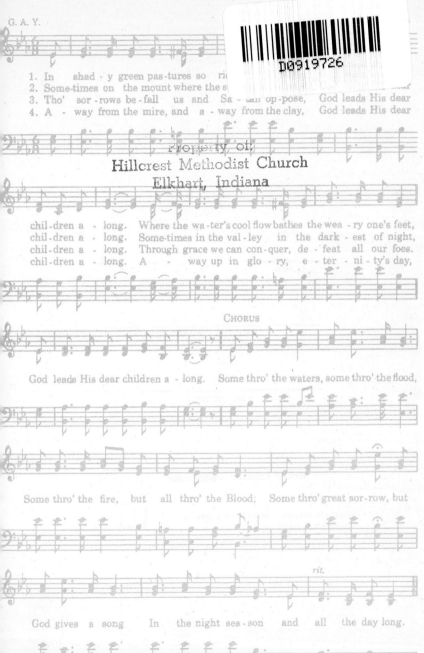

G. A. Y.

1. In shad - y green pas-tures so ri... God leads His dear
2. Some-times on the mount where the s... God leads His dear
3. Tho' sor - rows be - fall us and Sa - tan op-pose, God leads His dear
4. A - way from the mire, and a - way from the clay, God leads His dear

chil - dren a - long. Where the wa - ter's cool flow bathes the wea - ry one's feet,
chil - dren a - long. Some-times in the val - ley in the dark - est of night,
chil - dren a - long. Through grace we can con - quer, de - feat all our foes.
chil - dren a - long. A - way up in glo - ry, e - ter - ni - ty's day,

CHORUS

God leads His dear children a - long. Some thro' the waters, some thro' the flood,

Some thro' the fire, but all thro' the Blood; Some thro' great sor - row, but

rit.

God gives a song In the night sea - son and all the day long.

Dear Children

Dear Children

Hattie Larlham

Foreword by Kenneth H. Schmidt

HERALD PRESS
Scottdale, Pennsylvania
Kitchener, Ontario
1983

Library of Congress Cataloging in Publication Data

Larlham, Hattie, 1914-
   Dear children.

   1. Larlham, Hattie, 1914-   . 2. Nurses—Ohio—
Biography.   3. Handicapped children—Rehabilitation—
Ohio.   4. Handicapped children—Education—Ohio.
5. Hattie Larlham Foundation.   I. Title.
RT37.L34A34   1983   362.1'9892   82-25842
ISBN 0-8361-3325-0

DEAR CHILDREN
Copyright © 1983 by Herald Press, Scottdale, Pa. 15683
   Published simultaneously in Canada by Herald Press,
   Kitchener, Ont. N2G 4M5
Library of Congress Catalog Card Number: 82-25842
International Standard Book Number: 0-8361-3325-0
Printed in the United States of America
Design by Alice B. Shetler

83 84 85 86 87 88 10 9 8 7 6 5 4 3 2 1

To those
who
share our vision

Contents

Foreword

On rare occasions a true pioneer rises from among us and through sheer determination and singleness of purpose accomplishes a miracle that inspires us all.

Dear Children is the story of such a pioneer in our own times—the life story of Hattie Gadd Larlham as her intense energy propelled her from her roots in a West Virginia lay minister's family through nurses training; the ups, downs, and rootlessness of being married to a construction worker; away from and back to her faith in God.

She found her niche and life purpose in personally caring for severely developmentally disabled newborn. Her caring compassion for this neglected corner of humanity sparked the vision of her own family and a growing number of persons around her, eventually culminating in the development of the Hattie Larlham Foundation Hospital. Her influence has been felt by many segments of our society including governmental bodies.

Mennonite Voluntary Service personnel entered into the work in 1965 and the Mennonite Board of Missions assumed sponsorship of the program in 1977. We count it a real privilege to serve God in caring for these "dear children" and recommend this reading for your enlightenment, understanding, and inspiration!

Kenneth H. Schmidt, Director
Health and Welfare Department
Mennonite Board of Missions

One Step at a Time

The energy, the faith, the devotion which we bring to this endeavor will light our country and all who serve it, and the glow from that fire can truly light the world.

John F. Kennedy
Inaugural address
January 20, 1961

In shady green pastures so rich and so sweet,
God leads his dear children along;
Where the water's cool flow bathes the weary
     one's feet,
God leads his dear children along.*

Neighbors in the rural area of Portage County, Ohio, live acres apart, but we know each other well from the years of interdependence, from sharing our births and deaths and ills.

Jennie lived on a nearby farm. She and her husband were raising three children on a meager income, but like most of

---

* From the 1903 hymn by G. A. Young.

us they were survivors. Few calamities could break down the kind of people we were.

Jennie grew huge and round with her fourth child. As her time came, she was carted down to the county hospital in Ravenna, where I worked as a registered nurse.

In the delivery room the baby was born in silence. She didn't cry, even when spanked. She had no vocal cords.

The obstetrician, also a neighbor, spoke to all of us around the delivery table.

"Don't tell Jennie. She couldn't bear it."

> Sometimes on the mount where the sun shines
> so bright,
> God leads his dear children along.
> Sometimes in the valley, in darkest of
> night,
> God leads his dear children along.

The baby was profoundly damaged. Little Alice had no voice, and her head was too large for her tiny frail body. She didn't breathe very well. Her color was a dusky gray.

She was placed in a special-care unit, where the tense parents could watch her anxiously through a glass. Perhaps soon baby Alice would be released to their arms, they imagined, they hoped, they prayed.

They still didn't know Alice had already been categorized an inoperable hydrocephalic° by medical people—a ghoulish name for so helpless and silent a baby.

Alice began to suffer from tremors, like miniature earthquakes pounding to get out of her body. She spit up her food again and again. She swallowed less and less; we nurses

---

°Hydrocephally is a condition in a newborn baby in which the spinal canal fails to form correctly, diverting proper circulation of the spinal fluid which is then retained in the cranial cavity, enlarging the head and destroying mentality and body function.

hoped God would be merciful and shorten her days.

Finally the doctor inserted a feeding tube through Alice's flesh into her stomach, securing it there permanently. Still her body failed to grow. Her head, meanwhile, ballooned hideously.

I, the nurse, was also Jennie's friend and neighbor, so her questions came to me. Did I think Alice could see? Why was she not growing? Wasn't her head awfully large? Why didn't she ever cry? Why was she always trembling? Why couldn't she swallow anything? Why? Why? Why?

Alice remained in the hospital. By the time she was six months old her head was as big as a basketball. She no longer knew the comfort of being held. Terrible, wracking convulsions came at unexpected times. her helpless little body, held in the grip of some awful force, would lurch and writhe and sweat. The sterile tanks of pure oxygen must always be within quick reach, because she could cease to breathe in the midst of any attack. There could no longer be any doubt in the parents' minds about the seriousness of her condition.

As the permanency of Alice's state became increasingly apparent, Jennie grew more frantic, more desperate, more discouraged until at last she knew for a certainty what the doctor had lacked courage to tell her.

Insurance benefits had now been exhausted. Trying to maintain Alice in the hospital would deplete the family finances in a matter of days. No foster home would consider this pathetic, silent little scrap of humanity, although the parents cherished her.

To bring Alice home would rend the already frayed emotions of a family stretched to breaking by tragedy and poverty. Neither were the parents skilled enough to meet Alice's frightening medical needs.

Who would save this family from its tragedy? Once again

Jennie came to me with the questions I had no answers for. No easy solution existed. *I was not aware of facilities anywhere in the world for infants born with too many problems to be cared for at home.* The few medical institutions that had such capability cared only for "salvagable children." Our state facilities were not equipped to handle in-depth medical problems. In any circumstance they would not accept a child under six years of age. *There were no public assistance programs in any of our state agencies for a baby who had no potential to become a useful member of society.*

There was no source of help.

I had seen Alices before, many Alices. In many years as an obstetrical nurse I attended the births of dozens of hopeless babies—the ones labeled "nonsalvageable." I knew the frequent pattern. When the desperate parents ran out of money, the baby was discharged to go home with parents unequipped to care for it. There was no choice. Sometimes death came quickly, leaving guilt-ridden parents to reproach themselves for their inadequacy and for having given life to such an unfortunate one to begin with.

Some hopelessly damaged infants live on, sometimes destroying their families as the stress within the household over a period of time grows too great to bear. The siblings find themselves deprived of parental love and attention as the strange one demands minute-by-minute care. The mother and father, pressed to meet the colossal needs of the baby—and those of the other children as well—may become resentful and accusatory toward one another.

There are few if any eager babysitters. Social life disappears. The burden is the parents' alone, a wretched, tragic thing of their own biological making. Arguments frequently erupt in the tension. Fatigue and desperation add to the burden. A different set of questions begin to surface. What did *you* do to make this happen? Who is responsible? Why were we chosen for such a life? Why don't you take some of this pressure off of me?

The husband may quit coming home for dinner in the evening. Constant conflict may twist into hatred, psychosis, drinking, or worse. For some, love turns into grim endurance, and endurance rarely lasts forever. Often there appear to be no tangible rewards, no hope, nothing for the besieged parents of the nonsalvageable child to grasp onto.

Alice besieged me in her own way. Day after day I stood at her crib in the hospital ward. No one rushed to her when she cried, for her tears were soundless. She could not lift her huge, heavy head, so she winced and stretched her mouth and screamed in silence, like a tragic, tiny silent movie.

Something had to be done. Jennie's emotional framework was disintegrating as the dollars disappeared into the hospital's account books. Soon, when the money ran out, the hospital management would insist that Alice be moved out, and then . . . .

I prayed about the problem, taking it home with me each night to our farmhouse at the top of the hill.

"What can people do?" I asked myself out loud as I sat with my family one evening. "Why doesn't someone *do something?*"

"Aren't we someone?" my son Charles asked, as he looked at me seriously. He was a high school senior, a gentle boy, sensitive beyond his years. His question stopped me in my mental tracks. The next day I called the welfare agency to ask about licensing, and the wheels began to turn.

My husband, Dick, an operating engineer, raised his eyebrows. Hassling heavy machinery twelve hours a day, he had little strength left when he came home at night. He wasn't too sure about doing "this thing." Our youngest son, Giles, who ran headlong into life and had spent considerable

15

time in hospitals because of his impetuousness, told me directly that he didn't want his home "smelling of antiseptics." Lyndella, our thirteen-year-old daughter, was noncommittal. The chief pediatrician at the hospital considered it a shame that I would quit my job for this.

"Damn shame to lose a good hospital nurse," he fumed.

The day came, however, when the hospital bill was no longer being paid. Then the same doctor said to me, "If you're going to do this thing, why don't you take Alice home?"

We carefully explained to Jenny and her husband that Alice might die in our home at any moment of the day or night—while I slept, or during a visit to the bathroom. But I could make her comfortable as long as she could support life.

They accepted all of that.

It was an appropriately sunny day in June when Alice moved out of the hospital and headed for our farmhouse,

We brought Alice home to our farmhouse at the top of the hill.

her great head cradled in my lap. On the way home we stopped to introduce Alice to my mother and sister. They predicted disaster. I had quit a good-paying job at the hospital, they pointed out, in exchange for a monthly welfare check of $125.00. The welfare agency would also pay for the oxygen. The rest of the battle would be mine.

> Though sorrows befall us, and Satan oppose,
> God leads his dear children along;
> Through grace we can conquer, defeat all
> our foes,
> God leads his dear children along.

Life as we had known it was exchanged for a world which revolved around Alice.

In the evening, I pulled Alice's bed close to mine. Every night for the next two years, I slept with my hand against her body.

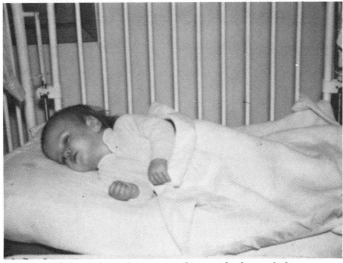

Life for us changed. Now everything revolved around Alice.

Alice became our princess, a beloved baby, our silent visitor. Our lives were governed by our love for Alice. Dick, who has always been inordinately fond of children, fell in love with her. Giles, with no antiseptic smells to drive him off, spent a lot of time beside her crib. He was growing up. Vulnerable Charles became her closest brother. Lyndella called her "our special angel."

"It takes so little to dry her tears," Lyndella wrote in a journal. "Just let her grasp your thumb. Her life is dependent on love. It makes you misty just to be near her."

Alice became our princess, a beloved baby, our silent visitor.

Alice gave us much we had not had before.

Even so, young as she was, Lyndella sensed the grim reality of caring for Alice. She had nightmares of dropping Alice and seeing her huge head shatter, like Humpty-Dumpty. She understood that soon Alice would be gone.

After Alice left us she wrote, "You have always known . . . that she would return to her Father, for she was yours for only a little while. As a part of you will go, a part of her is yours forever. She has drawn you closer to her home."

Alice edged her way into the hearts of five Larlhams—and *everybody* else who passed through that old farmhouse during the next two years.

Alice was the beginning. We had Alice, and a license from the Portage County Children's Service Board for nine more special babies. However, we had no equipment, no supplies, no resources—nothing except our faith in God.

Some through the waters, some through the flood,
Some through the fire, but all through the blood;
Some through great sorrow, but God gives a song,
In the night season and all the day long.

Had I known what lay ahead, I would surely have cowered in fear. The days stretching into the future lay like tangled underbrush, a region unexplored, impassable except for a singular straight path, hewn out by the hand of the Father.

. . . God leads his dear children along.

We were to follow one hesitant step at a time.

2
Through Troubled Water

We (that's my ship and I) took off rather suddenly. We had a report somewhere around four o'clock in the afternoon before that the weather would be fine, so we thought we would try it.

Charles A. Lindbergh
"Lindbergh's Own Story"
The New York Times
May 23, 1927

Wretchedly unattractive child that I must have been, I am sure I was dear to my devout, humble mountain parents. I basked in the warm glow of love permeating every corner of our home and every crevice of our meager existence. I was the youngest of eleven children in the home of a lay minister in the hills of West Virginia, and I truly felt as a dear child should feel: precious, loved, cherished, and protected.

Dad and Mom, in their close relationship to God, made his presence in our home real to each of us.

Dad, an ordained lay minister in the Evangelical United Brethren Conference, assisted the overburdened local minister as needed. He was often called upon to "ride the circuit," consisting of eight widely separated appointments, carrying out the regular duties of the absent pastor—preaching, teaching, counseling in time of trouble, performing weddings, and burying the dead. In the meantime, Mom, a sturdy, indomitable mountain woman, helped us children manage the farm and looked after her own household, while caring for the sick and birthing babies in surrounding mountain homes. Our parents taught us through Scripture and by example the satisfaction of achievement, the joy of service, and the results of sharing.

The corn bread and buttermilk served for supper—and mush for breakfast, with wild bee honey, or sorghum molasses—were food fit for a king, because they were shared in an atmosphere of love. Who needed more? Who needed an extra change of clothing—who could wear more than one outfit at a time anyway? The four-square house atop the hill was tight against winter winds, and we lay close to keep each other warm on our feather ticks at night. We were content.

Our numbers inevitably dwindled. My older brothers married. Ella went to Ohio to live with Mom's sister. She fell in love with the foster son of a farmer and married him. Gertrude wanted to teach, and somewhere the money was found for "normal school," over at West Liberty.

I began to dream of faraway places—the mission field—maybe Korea! That seemed like a glamorous career for a shy Christian girl who was much too tall (5' 10") and thin (118 pounds) to attract the local boys. Perhaps getting into the wide, wide world held special attractions for an awkward, self-conscious child who read voraciously rather than seek youthful friendships. There was so much to learn, and I had an eager, questing mind.

Even at an early age I had a deep sense of wanting to do something worthwhile for God and humanity. I wanted my life to have purpose and achievement. And if I could do that

21

Mom was a strong, indomitable mountain woman who helped with the farm work.

My childhood home was this four-square farmhouse atop Eight-Mile Ridge in Wetzel County, West Virginia.

beyond the hilly confines of Wetzel County, West Virginia—where Dad dispensed welfare supplies along with the gospel, while Mom and the rest of us ran the farm—that would be fine with me. Much as I loved my family, I didn't realize what the really good things in life were.

I would travel far before such knowledge could be acquired. Often I listened as spiritual matters were discussed at our big table. They were thought-provoking and many times far beyond my understanding, but I remembered them later.

One night the Scripture for family devotions was about the call of Samuel. The impressive old minister, an official from denominational headquarters who was spending the night at our farmhouse, asked us children, "What would you do if God were to speak audibly to you?" It was an exciting question that distinctly troubled me. A little shiver of fear ran down my back. Would God call me? How could his call be clearly recognized? Would I answer if he called? How?

I would need to know soon. Growing and learning in Wetzel County also meant observing and absorbing strange manifestations of God's power that marked local revival services—which sometimes extended throughout the winter.

Aunt Martha Jane pacing the aisles holding live coals in her extended palm without coming to harm. Grandma Higgins walking the backs of pews as she praised God. Cousin Lee Gadd, the blasphemer, who after he accepted Christ appeared to float weightlessly over the altar and back through the congregation, to draw companions to the altar to seek forgiveness from their sins. To see the power of God demonstrated visually, as the Holy Spirit witnessed in changed lives, was exciting. The witness of Christian attitude in daily Christian living, as neighbors assisted each other in times of hardship and trouble, was even more convincing of God's power.

For all the enthusiasm of the godly during revival, there was an equal amount of demonstration on the part of the godless. Like Lee, who before his conviction would sit through a service unmoved and later mount a tree stump to preach mockery as the Christians walked home. After his conversion, Lee became one of the most successful lay workers in our community. (Throughout his life he spoke of his uncle Charlie, my dad, as his guiding light.) How fortunate for me to have had such a one for a father.

Who can say how far a shadow reaches? Through how many generations does a planted seed reproduce itself to continue bearing fruit? I was to learn the answer later—much later.

Examples like cousin Lee brought God and his holy hosts close to us. The devil and his imps were just as real. I had op-

Myself as a young girl.

Dad, an ordained lay minister.

portunity to see the effects of both in the lives of the people around me. Early in my own life I decided which Master I wanted to follow. My nebulous dream of serving God in the mission field began to acquire substance. *I would like to be a nurse.*

Because my early childhood was peaceful, hopeful, fanciful, I came to believe that it should be so for all children. The devastated children I came to cherish later in life were never to have such opportunity. Even in the womb, they were stricken with monstrous life-burdens.

Later God would give me a son who could write of this. The lines of "Children's Song," written after the death of his brother's third baby vividly express the tumult of emotions that go hand-in-hand with the life work for which God had started preparing me.

CHILDREN'S
SONG

A child lies today
Under sentence of death.
For him there will be no pardon;
Commutation perhaps, to life—
Imprisoned within a twisted body
  and his unknowing mind.
The hope he never knew he had;
Blasted—

Children should not die, my friend,
Nor spend their lives imprisoned so.
Those fates should be reserved
For us. We've had a childhood;
Youth; a chance to live;
To hope and laugh; and love.
If we cannot promise him the same,
We can give him love,
And maybe see him smile.

25

Undeserved guilt that flies keening
Through the shivered lives
Of those who loved him first,
Must yield to hope.
Ours to gather in despairing shards
Of families, and say,
"I never knew him,
But I loved him.
He was my brother's child."

—*R. C. Larlham*

My own peaceful childhood ended abruptly the day news came to me at school that Dad had gone to be with God. Dad had promised to pick me up after school; we were to go to New Martinsville to get my high school graduation clothes. He had been so well. Even at 73 years of age he had been my active counselor and companion.

Somehow I had not considered that God might call him home to rest so soon.

Graduation was a bitter time. I felt no joy at the honor given me as valedictorian of my class, nor at the scholarship offered by Boanbrake Seminary. "Your father would have been so pleased" was an empty phrase. I knew he would indeed not have been pleased with me, because in those hours rebellion began brewing in my heart. I didn't want the scholarship. Neither did I accept my sister Gertrude's offer to help with expenses at West Virginia University in Morgantown, where I could have become a teacher.

I wanted to go away—alone. I wanted to break away from my past and forge a new exciting future. I wanted to become a registered nurse, although in those days nurses were reputed to be immoral, worldly women. (I knew this was not necessarily so. Nothing in my estimation could be greater than serving God as a medical missionary.)

My instincts were right for that field. I had helped Mom during a community epidemic of diphtheria, and found it satisfied me to cool fevered bodies and bring comfort to dying souls. God was speaking to me just as surely as he had spoken to Samuel that night in Eli's home. I must do the bidding of my heavenly Father. I believed my earthly father would have approved too. To satisfy myself on that point I had put out a fleece (Judges 6:37-40), asking God to reveal his will to me. When I dreamed three successive nights that Dad came and smiled upon me, I was convinced that what I had in mind was what I must do.

Soon after graduation I went to Ohio where I found work in a woolen mill. The wages were poor and the work hard, but I would be able to pay tuition and buy uniforms and books for the first year of training at the school of my choice. Edna and her husband, Orville, were glad to have me live with them. She had gone to Ravenna with her husband whose work took him away from home a great deal. During my years of nurse's training, they were my parents away from home; their home was my home.

City life in Youngstown, Ohio, was a strange new experience for me. It was like going abroad. The hospital life was totally different from any experience I had ever known. The city itself was made up of a conglomerate of second generation Europeans who had come there to work in the steel mills. My fellow students were largely representative of immigrant families from Poland, Austria, Hungary, and many of the Balkan States, Albania, Bulgaria, Greece, Yugoslavia. It was a time of learning much about peoples of other countries and how to relate to them.

The years of training brought new kinds of pressure—the responsibility of holding life in my own hands as a medical nurse. I fought a great fear of cutting off a life through some error in judgment. I also found there was plenty of fun to be had in the city, and periods of rebellion occurred and reoccurred with increasing frequency.

I wanted popularity, like that of my roommate who dated the interns, sneaked out to dance all night, and drank alcohol from the sterilizing trays. I learned to dress fashionably and how to deceive those around me. It became easy to neglect prayer and Bible reading. The movies and novels became more exciting and intriguing. Liquor gave me courage I had never known before. I learned to push fear behind me. Eventually I even lost my fear of making a mistake as a surgical assistant. I was in fact learning much more than I realized. I learned "the way of the transgressor." Like Jonah of old I disregarded God's command as I purchased my "ticket to Joppa" (Jonah 1:3) and for several years walked in spiritually dark places. The light had gone out of my life.

Nursing would have been immensely satisfying had I not indentured myself to the devil. But having once known a better way, and with my father's shadow falling long and true across my path, there was no fulfillment in my years of service.

Still pretending to be a Christian, I could not fool God. I discovered hypocrisy—and practiced it—quite successfully. Perhaps I even convinced myself for a time that things were going right.

God, however, is not mocked. "Whatsoever a man soweth, that shall he also reap" (Galatians 6:7). I was sowing a fine bed of nettles. I would later reap in sorrow as I sought a place of repentance.

Graduation from nurse's training came. After passing "state boards," I went to Ravenna, Ohio, where a job awaited me at the little forty-bed county hospital. Dr. Hoffman, a family friend, had given me a good reference. God was still working in my life in spite of me! Before long, I was placed in charge of an eight-bed orthopedic division.

Then one day a young operating engineer from New York, who had been working with tank builders, was admitted to my ward. Here was a different kind of person whose dreams were totally foreign to me. This cocky little Limey had fought and brawled to make a place for himself in a rough-and-tumble world dominated by bigger men. He was tense, rough-talking, and apparently fearless. I was simultaneously impressed, repelled, and magnetized.

Before the young man left my ward for New York City, I had handed in my resignation and went to Denver, Colorado, where I planned to enter medical school to become a doctor. I never enrolled, however. Instead I took a job at Denver General Hospital in the 48-hour postoperative center, a forerunner of intensive care as we know it today. It was tremendously exciting to see this kind of advance in patient care and to be a part of it.

The strange alchemy of love, however, drew me irresistibly back east. After six months I left my job and headed back east on a train bound for New York City. No longer the shy little mountain girl, I soon obtained a supervisory position in the 75-bed neurological division of Welfare Hospital on Welfare Island. Although I didn't realize it then, God was training me for the future. The hospital, directly affiliated with Cornell University, was deeply involved with central nervous system research. Less than a year later Dick Larlham and I were married there, laying the foundation for one of the oddest and yet somehow most productive unions God ever ordained.

New York was *Fun City*, and in my mind-set at the time it should have been great. But Dick was seldom home, traveling wherever his job took him. After a time I missed him greatly. I had not come halfway across a continent to be alone. Soon we were traveling together. Here the odd mixture began to show itself. In truth, there was no mixture at all. It was like trying to combine oil and water, quicksand and mercury.

We were madly in love, but the difference in temperament and background kept the waters of our life roiled and muddy. He understood my needs and longings no better than I understood his.

Nevertheless, in their own way, the next five years were good ones.

Dick and I were having a blast, as the world knew it. We went to parties, movies, dances, nightclubs—whatever came to hand—wherever his work was. There were no inhibitions. Swimming in the ocean or crabbing on the Hudson River—cooking clams at midnight in Boston and attending graduation at West Point—going to the art gallery on Madison Avenue and slumming in Greenwich Village—there was no end to the diversions we could find. Good summers came when work was plentiful, and lean winters followed when there was only enough money for liquor and poker. We were often hungry, sometimes cold too.

As a child I had become a good marksman hunting squirrels and woodchucks in the West Virginia hills with my dad. Dick and I had this in common. Often his trapline and our guns provided us with winter meat.

Home was wherever we chanced to be. It was a strange and different life. Exciting? Yes, but often very lonely.

I had nothing in common with the women I met from strange walks of life or the men who invaded our home. Dick's two big rowdy brothers shared our small apartments. Tank builders flocked to our quarters—Little Joe (so-called because he was so big); White Horse the Indian; Booger Red, the gambler; and many others—men who lived dangerously and worked hard during the day and spent their evenings playing cards and drinking. Lonely fellows who respected a good woman with a listening ear.

I learned a new vocabulary I had no use for. I prepared huge manly quantities of food when the funds were

Dick, a tank builder from New York, was admitted to my ward.

I graduated from nursing school and took a job at Ravenna, Ohio.

Less than a year later, Dick Larlham and I were married.

Dick and I were having a blast. There were no inhibitions.

31

available, and served boiled potatoes or hot porridge when money was scarce. For the first time in my life, I felt at ease with fellows . . . and learned that men and women have many of the same sensitivities.

During the five years on the road, while Dick worked on construction, I had three miscarriages. The odd mixture of Dick Larlham and Hattie Gadd had brought joy, sorrow, deprivation . . . and lessons from some of life's hardest schools.

After the disaster to the third child within me, I realized I could not bring a child into the kind of life we were living. As I reviewed the past several years, my thoughts were drawn continually toward God. It was not difficult to see that I had sold my birthright for a good time, just as Esau sold his for a bowl of porridge (Genesis 25:31-34).

I soon began having nightmares about Dick's lost soul. I loved him and realized that his true nature—a warm, living spirit—lay submerged somewhere within him by the pressures of his life and work. At night my dreams always ended with Dick on the far side of a wide abyss. I could never quite get across to him before I awoke.

At this point in my life I finally turned to a concentrated prayer and faith effort, trying to find my way back into the grace of God. As I studied the book of Hebrews, the wonderful mercy God extends to us because of Jesus and his death on the cross became apparent to me. When I fully accepted God's forgiveness, I prayed that he would mold me for service in his kingdom.

I prayed for a family, thanking God for the baby I would have. I dedicated the life of that yet unconceived child to the Lord. I also began praying for my husband to accept Christ as his personal Savior. Having once again tasted of "the good things of life," I wanted them all.

Willful disobedience is not quickly or easily dispensed with. I had not finished paying for that "ticket to Joppa." It was at this time, as I prayed earnestly for my husband, that we began having serious problems in our marriage. Satan was not willing to give up easily.

By the time I gave birth to Charles, a beautiful, healthy, nine-pound boy, Dick had become distant and hostile. Communication had grown increasingly difficult. The fact that I was going to church regularly didn't help matters at all.

The baby and I went to church alone. I sought God's will in our lives, and, as he grew older, Charles too prayed for Daddy. Fourteen months after Charles' birth, Giles was born. He was a squalling, lusty, temperamental Larlham.

Those were war years. Dick was working in the shipyards as a union steward. His life was in constant jeopardy. We lived in government housing outside Chicago, on a flooded river bottom where the ice was eight inches thick and the wind blew constantly through our thin walls as if they were straw.

The babies were always sick. There were no affordable medical services. I thanked God for my nursing skills when Giles had severe asthma attacks which resulted in terrifying croup. There were long nights when it seemed he would surely asphyxiate. I skated to the grocery store, pulling the babies on a sled. Life held less and less glamor.

God, however, knew our problems and he led us, his dear children, faithfully along.

When Dick had had enough, he left the shipyards in Chicago and went to South America to work for Standard Oil. He didn't choose to take us with him, so I returned with the boys to the bosom of my family. By this time Mom and my four sisters were living in Ravenna, Ohio, where we had many friends who attended the First Methodist Church.

Mom came to share my apartment when I applied for work again at the hospital where I had met Dick several years before. Knowing where God has led me since then, it seems odd that at that time I requested not to be assigned to the newborn nursery. I felt inadequate because it had been several years since I worked with newborns. Perhaps the memory of three miscarriages was still too painful too.

Nevertheless, God had his hand on me and upon my life; I was put in charge of a premature nursery unit, where I learned much that I would need to know later. As I clung to God's hand, although my grip was now timid and unsure, he led me down the path to my future.

> Some through the waters,
> Some through the flood,
> Some through the fire,
> But all through the blood.

I had family pictures made to remind my husband in Venezuela of his home in Ohio. Each night the little boys and I talked about Daddy. I was afraid they might forget about him. Although we had grown far apart, I still loved him. He was the father of our children and our marriage vows were sacred.

Then suddenly there was a military eruption in South America and Dick, along with many other North Americans, was evacuated. One afternoon while working in our tiny backyard garden, I looked up to see my husband coming down the path. I had received no word that he might be coming home. The sight of him was wonderful. God was working in our lives; my husband had returned. At that moment Dick's physical presence alone was enough to rekindle my waning faith.

Dick, fighting great spiritual battles, was sick of the construction field and unending travel. He felt ready to settle down and make a home for his family. That would not be easy because he had no experience in any other kind of work. We knew his educational background was too meager to qualify him for some of the better job opportunities. For the next several months, one unhappy job gave way to another in rapid succession. We moved, distraught with life, to a farmhouse, and asked Dick's widowed mother to spend some time with us. We needed her to care for the children so that I could keep working at the hospital until Dick found something worthwhile to do. But he and his mother didn't get along very well.

In January 1950 Lyndella arrived, all twelve pounds of her, grossly overweight because I had developed hypothyroidism during pregnancy. The delivery was a difficult one—really too much for me—and I couldn't go back to work. The next year was hard, but I had not yet learned all there was to know about hard times.

Another year came and went. It was January again, and I could no longer put off the major repair surgery I had needed since the birth of our last baby. Mother Larlham had long since returned to New York. Jobs were still not available for my husband and money for our needs was practically nonexistant. I knew what it was to pray and depend entirely on God. It was cold, and there was little coal for the furnace.

When I went to Youngstown to have surgery, my sisters took the children to care for them. Dick went to work as a pharmacy supply clerk for forty dollars a week. Pneumonia followed surgery, and then more serious lung problems developed. I had no choice except to go to Edwin Shaw Sanatorium for continuing treatment. The process of recovery was painfully slow and discouraging. Bronchiectasis made life a constant agony of coughing and gasping for breath. Finally the right lung had to be collapsed.

The more faithfully I prayed, it seemed, the more my life unraveled. I was surely reaping the harvest of what had been sown during those careless years. That verse in Galatians 6:7 came into my mind more and more frequently. "Be not deceived; God is not mocked. Whatsoever you sow, that shall you also reap." I was paying the full price of transgression.

During the spring following my surgery, Dick went to work on the afternoon shift in a machine shop in Bedford, Ohio. We had borrowed money from my sister Gertrude, for a down payment on a few acres of land and a rambly old house of nine huge rooms, plus an attic, basement, porch, and innumerable out-buildings—a wonderful place to rear a family. The little boys loved the woodlot, the babbling brook, the enormous maples in the front yard, and the old blind pony that came with the farm.

Entranced by the overgrown flower gardens, I set about making war on the weeds, while getting my required time in the sun. A little pony manure worked in around the rosebushes would, I thought, surely pay off in dividends of flowers.

When I went in to prepare lunch after a couple of hours of work, there were scratches on my hands. By 2:00 p.m. when Dick left for work, I thought I was coming down with a virus. My muscles were achy and I was fighting a terrible headache. Dick advised me to put the children to bed early, take a hot bath, and settle down for a good night's sleep. By 6:00 p.m., when I finished bathing the baby, I realized I had more to worry about than the possibility of a virus with my lung not yet entirely healed. I couldn't turn my head or bend over at all. Charles had to lift Lyndella out of the tub onto the bed and get her into her nightclothes. When it was time for the boys to go to bed, I couldn't climb the stairs. Six-year-old Charles was concerned about Mommy. Mommy knew she had something to be worried about.

I called my friend, a registered nurse who lived about two miles away, and asked her to come over. I could still talk.

She helped me up the stairs, got me into bed, and went downstairs. I heard the front door close behind her—and that was it! I couldn't believe she had left me alone with three small children, totally helpless in the grip of what I suspected might be tetanus. It would be years and years before I could let myself forgive her.

Sometime during the night, Charles awoke to my moaning. He came into the room, somehow pulled me into a sitting position, and got my feet on the floor, and pattered back to bed. There I sat—unable to move a muscle.

When Dick came home he was too exhausted to do anything but tumble into bed in his clothes, snoring almost before his head touched the pillow. Not wanting to awaken me, he had not even turned on the light. As for me, I could no longer ask for help.

When Charles came to my room in the morning, he could see that something had overwhelmed me. Unable to wake his father he dashed out in his sleepers and ran down the road to the nearest neighbor. The Gabelines came up, called an ambulance, and went with me to the hospital.

I shall never forget my despair or the terrible pain of muscle spasms as the awful vice of lockjaw (tetanus) gripped my entire body. My hands were drawn back on my forearms as my back arched higher and higher off the bed. I could not swallow and as time went on the agony in my throat seemed insufferable. Worse than the pain were the voices of the nurses and doctors I knew so well, talking about what a terrible death I was going to have. Finally Dr. Huffman suggested trying massive doses of cortisone.

One painful eternity followed another as my agony increased, while my mind remained unusually clear and alert. There was nothing I could do except concentrate on Scripture and pray. It was about 2:00 a.m. while concentrating on 1 Corinthians 10:13, that I began to relax and soon fell into blessed slumber.

Our pastor later told me he had called the church body to

convene in prayer. "Your little boys," he said, "were praying for Mommy at 2:00 a.m. when God heard and answered."

It was several weeks before I regained full capacity of my body. God must surely have a purpose in sparing my life, I told myself, and I was ready to listen to his call. My answer would be, "Here am I. I'm ready." That trip to Joppa was behind me. I had much to be grateful for.

Still recuperating the next summer, I joined a prayer group. My husband, feeling more insecure and frustrated than ever, became increasingly irritable, and discouraged.

The children and I went to church on the bus each Sunday praying that someday Daddy would join us. We were attending a small Baptist mission where the message was evangelistic, plain, and to the point. For a time we continued to go there alone. Then there came a Sunday when Daddy joined us. When the altar call was given Dick left the church weeping. On the way home he asked, "What's the matter with me?"

"The Holy Spirit has spoken to you," I answered simply.

The following Sunday morning he didn't wait for the invitation to be given. He hurried forward and gave his life to God. That afternoon nine bottles of liquor and a case of beer went down the drain. The need for them, and the problem, had been taken away—the desire was gone.

I had no illusions that all the problems were over. Some of the old habits would not be as easily eradicated but the beginning was encouraging. I believed that he who had began this good work in my husband was able to continue it. He could do exceedingly and abundantly over and above all that we could ask or expect. I knew my husband, too, and felt sure we could now walk together in the light of God's love.

There is not space in this narrative to relate how the grace of God sustained us in succeeding days as the devil tried to reclaim the soul of my beloved. There were days of darkness and troubled waters, but we could face them together because we had a common bond. At last we were both ready to do God's bidding. We were ready for Alice . . . and more.

3
A Mission at Home

Out of the mouths of babes and sucklings hast thou ordained
strength.

Psalm 8:2

"Larry Bird" is our completely adorable, unpredictable,
lovable little fellow of whom we are apt to say, "Have you
seen Larry? He was right here just a minute ago. Look
quick, so he doesn't wander away and get hurt."

One day as I was tending Alice, our first so-called "nonsalvageable," I looked up to see a huge man towering over me.
I had not heard him come in.

"Will you take Larry?" he asked.

Larry's father was a Cleveland policeman whose wife was
under psychiatric care. For two years she had spent 24 hours
a day anticipating every need of her totally helpless child.
She could stand no more. I explained to the daddy my need
for another crib (this prudently became part of our admission fee thereafter). The next day Larry joined our family
and began winding himself around our hearts as he grew,

and we saw resources developing that the doctors had said he wouldn't have!

First of all, Larry had crippled feet; the tendons were not attached to his ankle bones at birth and the doctors never expected him to walk at all. Good orthopedic surgery took care of that, along with postoperative physical therapy.

"Have you seen Larry? I've put childproof locks high up on the doors, so he can't open them.

"Oh, there he is, halfway up the stairs, with our daughter Lyndella sneaking along behind to catch him if he loses his balance."

It doesn't matter where we have to follow Larry, just so long as we know that he is safe. He is learning to get around. I remember the day he got into my paste when I was laying floor tile. He rubbed it into his hair! What a mess.

Another day he climbed into the bathtub with all his clothes on, and turned on the faucets. He can beat me to the mop bucket almost every time, too. Just yesterday he discovered that he can climb into an easy chair and turn the lights on and off. I found him there squealing, "Whee . . . whee . . . whee . . .! All of that is especially thrilling to us, because Larry was stamped "nonsalvageable" when he came to live in our home.

Nowadays "Larry Bird" is so active that it's a full-time job just keeping up with him. That's cute for any one-year-old— except that Larry is three.

When he came to live with us at the age of two, his father had just been told by the neurologist that Larry would probably never have a mentality beyond that of an infant four months old. He was afflicted by severe attacks of epileptic seizures. Medication now has those under control and Larry is catching up fast. He is fond of clambering into Dick's lap and saying, "Hi, Dick!" and then he extends a chubby little hand to show off whatever he has found along the way. He often looks up at me as I drink my morning coffee to inquire, "Mommy's bottle?" We nearly burst with pride and happiness because *we know his mind is working*.

"Have you seen Larry?"

"Yes, I have seen Larry. There he is—playing ball."

That day will surely come. *He has taught us that not every nonsalvageable child is hopeless.* We are learning that early diagnostic evaluations that write a child off are not always reliable.

We have learned, too, that parents are hungry for someone to talk to. In such sensitive conversations we have found that it is easy to speak of God and his great mercy. Invariably we hear parents ask, "Why did this happen to me?" It is the age-old problem of *self*. In every parent we see the need for self to die and let God's love fill a broken heart. *Our mission field lies right here in our own home*.

The next guest to arrive at the farmhouse was Jamie, our darling little newborn. It may well be that darling Jamie was *the* missionary baby. He probably led many more souls to Christ than any of us who cared for him.

It was Jamie who touched the heart of the visiting banker, Rudolph Garfield. Mr. Garfield, the great-grandson of President James A. Garfield, heard of our work and came from Cleveland to see what was going on. He was weeping when he left Jamie's bed. Turning at the door, he said, "I want to help." God's ways are beyond our understanding. Mr. Garfield had a profound impact on our work both financially and emotionally; we will always be grateful for his interest.

As Jamie's head grew in size, because of the anatomical problem of hydrocephaly, it filled a 32-inch crib. No one could cuddle him—he was trapped.

In addition to being a hydrocephalic, Jamie was paralyzed from the waist down, his little legs and feet were misshapen, and he couldn't see. Eventually it became terribly difficult to turn him in his crib because of the paralysis and because of the size and weight of his head. The night aide called me every two hours to help her change his position. I couldn't keep doing this, so I told her God would help her if she asked.

Soon there came a night when she didn't call. The next morning she told me, "I didn't want to call you. I couldn't turn Jamie last night and so I prayed, but I knew so little about prayer that it didn't work.

"Then I just fell on my knees and said, 'God, Mrs. Larlham said you would help if I asked.' I knew I couldn't turn Jamie myself but I tried anyway, and it was easy; then I realized God could forgive my sins if I asked. Praise his name: I asked, and he did!

"Oh, I just love Jamie!" she added.

Her joy was complete. Love flooded her soul. She had found Christ through her relationship with one of his precious children. I have seen this happen time and time again, for God's hand is in this work.

Jamie lived with us five years, a hydrocephalic with myelomeningocele, bilateral hernias, and club feet and total lack of eyesight. During those five years he taught us many things we didn't know before. He rarely cried, but if he murmured we knew something was needed, and he had small words for answering questions.

"Are you wet, Jamie?"
"Un-huh."
"Are you tired, Jamie?"
"Huh-uh."
It took very little to make him happy.
Lyndella wrote of him in her journal:

Jamie's little hands are possibly the most beautiful things I have ever seen.

>When he is asleep they lie curled up like little seashells; when he is happy they are opening rosebuds. The grasp of Jamie's little fingers holds all the love and confidence there is. When he is in pain, they express all of the world's agony.
>
>Jamie is not just any baby—he has become MY baby. I am sure that your baby is completely adorable and beautiful, but Jamie's little hands are the only perfect part God gave to his little body.
>
>Little Jamie can't see, but he knows our voices and is delighted with the nearness of those he loves.
>
>Although we cannot pick him up, the grasp of his little fingers tells me of his love for me too.

Jamie's patience wrung our hearts. As he became more and more trapped by his gross distortion, I resolved never again to tolerate this kind of affliction if it could possibly be prevented. Jamie went home to heaven on Christmas Day. We rejoice to know he has perfection in heaven but we still miss him.

Jamie taught us one more thing: *It's important to begin intervention early!*

It is essential that the condition of a newborn infant be evaluated immediately, if possible, so that necessary mental and physical stimulation may be instituted at once. Jamie's many problems led us into a philosophy and policy that calls for early developmental training and stimulation. Much of today's sophisticated methodology in this field was anticipated during those early days of close observation and intensive work with the profoundly devastated infants who enchanted us in our farmhouse.

Dr. Lang, my old boss from the hospital, attended our babies. Our neighbor and family physician, Dr. Ed Knowlton, came over when there was an emergency. Dr. George Sprogus from Hiram College began talking about research. God led us into many paths of reward.

Soon there was Cocoa, a quadriplegic spastic baby who screamed for hours on end without stopping. Cocoa had

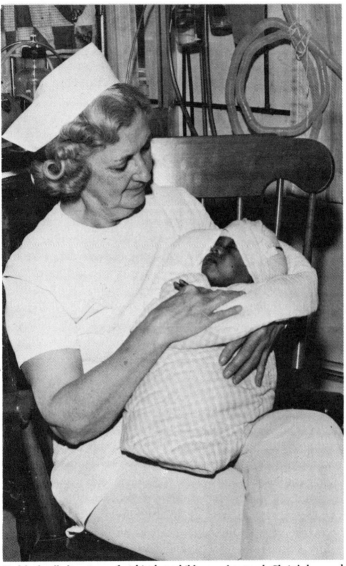

God had called us to comfort his dear children and to teach Christ's love and saving grace to their parents. That would be our purpose.

been left on a bench in the Terminal Tower in Cleveland. A search began for her parents—a search which ultimately ended in Chicago. Cocoa became our first public relations agent, as the message of her plight and our services was carried by word of mouth across the country. That message was, "*Someone cares.*"

Truly the devil is a master at producing misery. Dear little Becky, two years old, had been hideously molested by her father. As Becky rocked endlessly and murmured, "Pretty Becky," we prayed for the depraved creature who had destroyed her. Becky never recovered. We did get her to smile before she left this earth. Thereafter, we believe she saw the compassionate, loving face of God and that erased her pain.

Then there was Roberta, whose uncle talked to us about euthanasia. "It's unfair to my sister," he said, "to be burdened with this continuing concern."

When challenged to administer the lethal drug himself, his refuge was, "I'm not a nurse."

And there, through little Roberta, another philosophy was born. *What constitutes undue preservation of life?* When are we outside the will of God?

Dick and I, along with the parents and our medical staff, had to come to grips with those questions during the early days of our service. Little Roberta helped us decide. We determined to bring every measure of comfort possible to the child without going to extremes of lifesaving. This still left many questions unanswered.

If surgery brings relief but lengthens a seemingly hopeless life, then what?

Do we give antibiotics if there is no hope for life fulfillment?

Will we resort to the use of oxygen?

Should a child starve when a feeding tube could sustain it?

Ultimately, every question was resolved with prayer alone. One Scripture impressed us in particular. It is found in Job 1:21. "The Lord gave, and the Lord hath taken away; blessed be the name of the Lord."

We had no right to play God. He had called us to comfort his dear children and to teach Christ's love and saving grace to their parents. That would be our purpose.

The farmhouse was becoming crowded. When Dr. Myron Owen brought Charity directly to us from the delivery room, wrapped in a blanket, she was only three hours old. Charity's entire body was a mass of tumors. One eye was missing. Her heart had only three chambers instead of four. There was only one kidney. What further damage she may have sustained we never knew.

Myron had been a resident doctor during my days as a student nurse at Youngstown, and I remembered the tenderness of his heart. "Let's be kind," he said. "Don't put her

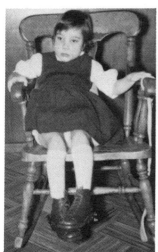

Two-year-old Becky had been hideously molested by her father.

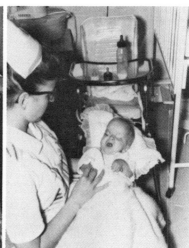

Charity stayed with us for two years.

into oxygen." We didn't, but we did tube-feed her, and we purchased an alternating pressure mattress for her little crib. The softest blankets were selected to keep her warm. When she developed a streptococci infection, we gave her penicillin to relieve the misery caused by a sore throat.

Charity stayed with us two years, almost daily helping us define our mission. These were rewarding years, because we saw her parents gain the courage to try again. Before Charity went away, there was a baby brother to take her place in their hearts. And through Charity they had gained an inheritance in heaven. Those parents now have an expectancy no one can take away. They cannot be sure of eternal life for the son remaining with them, where Satan's snares are set on every hand—but they can have the assurance of Charity's eternal joy—and health. They know, too, that they can someday go to be with her forever.

We turned some families down who were capable of caring for their children at home, but preferred not to do so. Dear little mongoloid babies could be an endless joy, with their great capacity to love and their need to be sheltered and shared. Cerebral-palsied children, who often have great intellect trying to break through their physical barriers, are beautiful—but not part of our mission. For those parents we provided a home trainer to assist them in learning how to cope with the needs of the special child in their midst. The blind and deaf children, who need highly specialized training, are precious but we could not accept them. We began to establish policies regarding the kinds of children for whom we could provide the most appropriate and needed care.

Ours would be a service to newborn infants with devastating problems. The family most in need of respite would be given first consideration if we were forced to choose between two children whose needs seemed equally great.

Our family was growing ... Alice, Jamie, Cocoa, Becky, Larry, Roberta, Charity ... our dear children. There were also my own three—Chuck, Giles, and "Bug" (Lyndella's unstoppable nickname). And, of course, there were Dick and myself. It was getting to be quite a household indeed! I knew that each of us were equally precious in the eyes of God.

And then there was sweet Sylvia.

Whether to be grateful for the opportunity to know about parental grief, remorse, love, and sorrow, or whether to be sorry that I ever met our "Silver Baby," is hard to know. This I do know: I will never be the same again, because with Sylvia came all of those heartrending emotions every parent

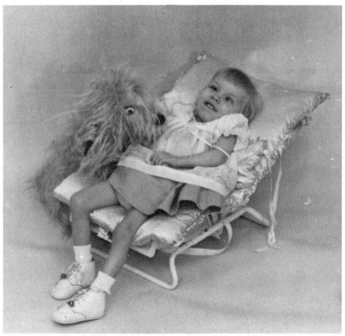

I will never be the same again because of Sylvia, our "Silver Baby."

of a handicapped child must surely experience. Although I did not give birth to Sylvia, she became as much mine as though she were my own flesh and blood.

When the social worker at Deaconess Hospital in Bay View Village called to ask us to care for tiny three-day-old Sylvia, she said, "This baby's parents can't manage her. They live in a small apartment with no modern facilities, and, although the mother is only 13 and the father 15, they have another baby just over a year old. The father works days at a filling station," she continued, "and sleeps nights at a lumberyard, where he acts as watchman."

It was inconceivable! Indeed this young couple trying desperately to survive needed help with the new baby because she had cystic fibrosis. She would spend much time in a micro-mist tent, to ease her breathing problems. She was also blind and severely palsied. Her flaccid arms and legs would never be of any use to her. I questioned even our own ability to care for this helpless little morsel of life whose problems were so enormous, but with God's help we would try.

It was a dreary spring morning, with intermittent snow and rain, when the local ambulance driver and I went to get the baby. *From the moment I first took her in my arms, she was mine.* From then on there was a closer bond between her and me than with any of our other babies. In infancy she would eat for no one but me. When she cried in the evening, I took her onto the porch where she could hear the baby frogs singing in our swamp. We called them "peepers." I spoke to her of the beauty of the night and crooned a lullaby walking back and forth as I cuddled her close to my body. I was the only mother she would ever know. As she grew older, she would lie quietly in her tent and listen for my footsteps....

We had you, precious, for twelve lovely years.

It has been six years since I last saw you, Sylvia, and I still dream of you ... running down the corridor to meet me, with arms outstretched and long silver tresses flying. A normal, well little girl, running to greet her mommy.... Your normal mind no longer encased in your poor helpless body.

I awake to realize my foolish dream....

Although completely inhibited by her palsied muscles and sightless eyes, Sylvia demonstrated a knowledge of what went on around her and communicated in her own way, obedient to commands and responsive to love, her sweet smile and laughter catching at the heartstrings of those who cared for her.

I wonder, Sylvia, did you find understanding where we entrusted you to others? Are you happy with them? I'm told you are, but I will never really know because I convinced myself it was best for you if I didn't visit. Was I thinking of you or of myself who couldn't bear it?

Sweet Sylvia, my silver baby, so utterly helpless—totally dependent. How could I justify to you, to myself, our final separation? Do you feel betrayed by the only one you trusted?

Dear God, please forgive me, it seemed I had no choice.

SWEET SYLVIA

As twilight falls hobgoblin
heads come tumbling out of
    closets.
Pain's voiceless cry
goes wandering into vacancy.

Angel wings laden with
stardust hover round your
    crib.
Be safe, sweet gentle child
who knows of sorrow.

Strange life without fulfillment,
whose laughter comes so swiftly,
like silver chimes.
Sweet music of the soul.

Because you cannot see, or run
    or speak,
my heart must break with sorrow.
I hold you close and weep,
for you and I and every lost
    tomorrow.

51

Christmas was coming, and our family continued to grow. We had emptied our small savings account and didn't know where to turn for help. Dick was out of work and wanted to take our own children to New York to visit their aged grandmother.

Giles decided to stay and help with the babies while Dick, Chuck, and Lyndella left to spend two weeks with Dick's mother Nina. The 15-pound Christmas ham they had splurged and sacrificed to buy was left behind in the excitement. After they drove away and disappeared into a December snowstorm, I remembered the ham taking up room in our small refrigerator. I burst into tears as I wondered what they would eat. There was only enough money to get them out there and back.

In the meantime Giles and I had our own problems. Seven babies! That was too many for one person to care for 24 hours a day. We didn't have enough income to hire more than one night aide. That meant I had to be up all night twice a week.

I felt my problems with staffing could be solved when the census reached eight. Then, with the small sum that each child's sponsors were giving, our budget could be stretched to employ a daytime assistant or a part-time night worker. Yet we couldn't pray for additional children with such horrendous problems as those already facing us in our seven occupied cribs!

"God, if there be those who need our help," we prayed hesitantly. "*Please make them aware of the good service we provide.*" Dick expressed it much more poetically.

> If there be those
> who need our care,
> help us with them
> our life to share.

That Christmas prayer took us into a strange, sad situation.

On Christmas Eve, Jonnie Patrick arrived wrapped in a diaper, carried in a shoebox by a sober black-robed sister from a hospital in Cleveland. As the softly falling snow whitened her robes, she introduced me to the newborn infant, 10 inches long and weighing only three pounds.

He had serious orthopedic problems. The baby's father had requested that the mother not be told the child had lived.

We never knew the baby's name. To us, little "Jonnie Patrick," as we dubbed him, was God's Christmas gift to us.

With no cervical vertebrae, his head sat directly on his little shoulders, but his face was beautiful. There was promise of golden curls on a well-shaped head.

Giles and I heated blankets and filled hot-water bottles for the clothes basket, which I placed on two chairs over the hot-air register. We hooked up a hot plate and started a steam kettle boiling to keep the air moist. I didn't want to lose our precious little premature baby. We had no way of ascertaining what great future Jonnie might have. He might have a perfectly normal mentality—it was certainly possible.

"Dear God," I prayed, "bring peace to the mother who has lost her baby on this Christmas Eve." As I worked, my thoughts turned to Bethlehem and the baby born on that Christmas Eve night. "God," I prayed again as I worked, "help us to bring that message of peace, which came two thousand years ago, to the despairing parents of these little children you have entrusted to our care."

I had found my mission field—not in foreign places, but right here in my own household. It would be my commission for God to teach at home; others would be called to carry the message into the uttermost parts of the world. That night my vision of the far-reaching effects of the ministry we had been called to perform began to unfold.

Jonnie Patrick didn't stay long. As he grew and developed, we knew our first hope would be realized. His responses were phenomenal. I called the hospital and asked to have Jonnie readmitted for orthopedic assessment. The orthopedic experts decided to operate immediately to see if Jonnie couldn't be helped to live a normal life and be returned to his parents to raise.

We never saw our bright little baby again. The same arms received him that had carried him to our door. "Jonnie will stay the night at the convent," said the sister as she picked him up, "and be admitted to the hospital tomorrow."

The next morning I received a call. Our little guy had died during the night, they told us. The sister made a weak attempt to console us: "Jonnie will make a beautiful angel," she said.

Suddenly I knew the heartbreak his mother had felt when she heard those words on Christmas morning.

We had learned something crucial about responsibility, however. *Never again would we admit a baby to any hospital or other facility without adequate referral and proper casework; never again would we trust our children to anyone except authorized persons. In fact, never again would we accept a child without identification.*

I shall always wonder where my Jonnie is. If he lived, who was there to help him over the hard places? Guilt would be my constant companion for many days to come.

Nursing I knew about. Love I could share in abundance. But there was so much more to learn, some of it difficult and painful. "Dear God, I'm not worthy," I prayed. "Please forgive me for letting Jonnie go." Of all the tragic little children who have died in our care, Jonnie Patrick is the only one I felt we really *lost*.

4
Comfort and Happiness

Winter finally spent itself that first year of our involvement with our special charges. Dick had been without work during the cold months, and had helped at home as much as he could. The children loved him and responded to his deep fatherly voice as they never had to mine. He was the only father most of them would ever know.

As spring approached, a new little arrival began growing and blossoming in Dick's particular kind of love and tenderness. Weedgie was a blond two-year-old little girl who, in her parents' home, had regressed to a prenatal state emotionally because she was the victim of what is known as the "battered child syndrome." At first Weedgie responded to no stimulus. For a long time, whenever we held her she exploded into violent seizures of fear, until Dick somehow turned the switch in her little mind and her feelings began to thaw.

Eventually she started eating and the feeding tube could be removed. We discovered that music had a soothing effect. It caused her to move—even though that movement at first was expressed in turning away toward the wall. Some of the tenseness was going away from her body. Later she would learn to hop backward like a bunny.

Lyndella, who loved Weedgie, wrote:

> She pulls at your heart until it nearly breaks. It takes so little to bring her joy, only a note or two of music. Pick her up and rock her—sing to her—and she snuggles happily into your shoulder.
>
> Blink your eyes, and the scamp is gone. Weedgie doesn't run or crawl away. She hops like a bunny rabbit. The only thing she's missing is a furry tail. She nibbles at everything and everyone, pulls hair, and scolds the water faucet for not turning on at her request.
>
> She loves water. If the right doors are not closed, you can always find her headfirst in the only liquid available to her—the toilet. With Weedgie around there is never a dull moment.
>
> In the evening she goes to sleep assured her job has been done, for she has thoroughly depleted the energy of every person within her special world.

Dr. Schomer, visual perception consultant from Cleveland, found her to have multiple visual disabilities, including inversion (she saw everything upside down). Work in the field of visual perception was just beginning. At the Hattie Larlham Foundation (which I will describe more fully later), Dr. Schomer developed many programs that would benefit children with learning disabilities due to faulty visual perception.

Weedgie had other problems. Her deep-seated fears would be more difficult to overcome.

Before long, Weedgie was Dick's special friend. When he

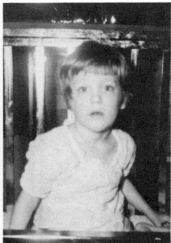

A victim of "battered child syndrome," Weedgie was Dick's special friend.

Louise had multiple visual disabilities as well as deep-seated fears.

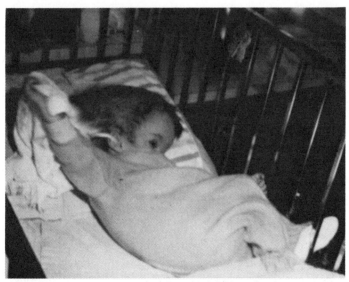

Society knew little about the profoundly disabled children who often were hidden in attics and dark basements. Ours were the faceless children of the world.

returned to work, she waited silently all day in her corner, hopping out when he came home, and leaning her face against his trouser leg. Soon it was clear that Weedgie needed us less than we needed her.

What she really needed was psychological help. We transferred her, after careful investigation, to a facility that could provide what she needed. Years later she came out of her strange world and began to relate to others.

Louise (the name she took) was found to have hidden herself from her fears in the closet of several personalities, even at that tender age. Today she is a brilliant, sensitive young lady.

Her mother was able to forget that she once had given life to a child. Her father remarked to us many years ago, "Her only problem is that she has not been beaten enough." How little he understood the most precious values in life. When Weedgie learned there are loving people in the world, she came to terms with her problems, conquering her early fear of life. Under psychiatric care her multiple personalities disappeared to release a charming intelligent child.

Meanwhile, my husband, the children, and I lived a close life, sharing responsibilities as we cared for those who needed us. We came to know and understand each other better than most family members ever do. Lyndella loved to help with supper. She acquired a joy in food preparation that has been a pleasure to her all through her life. Dick was marvelous in soothing those who were distressed. He massaged and compressed little Cocoa's legs when she screamed with pain from muscle spasms. Giles helped with cleaning up and doing extras around the house. Charles, now in college, set up a study corner in the children's rooms and watched over them while I slept in the evenings. It was a wonderful time of sharing. We were supremely happy— five Larlhams committed to a single purpose.

They were good days; fun was not lacking. One evening when our washer refused to work, Charles and Lyndella took the clothes—including huge sacks of diapers—to the local laundromat. A gullible lady, seeing the dozens of diapers, assumed the two were a prolific young husband and wife. "How many children have you?" she inquired, a little wide-eyed.

"Eight," Lyndella promptly replied, seizing the golden opportunity.

"Oh! And you are both so young," said the lady with a touch of wonder in her voice. "Are they boys or girls?"

"Well," replied Chuck quite casually, "some of each." He thought a moment and then added, "And Cocoa is black, you know."

Alas, the woman turned out to be a bigot. She was overcome with horror and disgust at what they seemed to be telling her. At that point, Charles and Lyndella relented and explained our service to her.

Sadness, of course, had to come too. The roses could not bloom forever. As our sons approached manhood there was much talk of protection of home and loyalty to one's country. Civic pressures were strong.

One Sunday night after a youth meeting at church, Giles surprised us. "Mom, Dad, I've enlisted in the armed forces."

We talked far into the night. Finally, Charles, a first-year college premed student, said, "I've made up my mind. If little brother goes, I go too." That was Charles, always thinking first of someone else. "We'll go by the buddy system and not be separated," he added.

A week later they were at Fort Knox.

I never saw them as boys again. When they came home three years later they were men I scarcely knew. I felt the heartache and sadness that comes when some other force usurps parental influence.

Giles was barely 18 years old when he came home from boot camp the first time. I asked about their training.

"Well," he said, "I know fifteen different ways to kill a man." As a boy he had learned the Sermon on the Mount and the Ten Commandments at my side, but now he sat there a man who had mastered 15 ways to kill a fellow human. I had no words for this stranger whose new life I could not relate to.

Life at home for Dick, Lyndella, and me would never be the same. A sad loss had come to us, but our loneliness drew us ever closer together. We found ourselves sharing more intimately our thoughts, joys, and sorrows. It was hard, however, to accept the scriptural admonition that we must learn to be thankful for all things (Ephesians 5:20). I could not at that time find it in my heart to be thankful for what was happening in the lives of our sons.

Charles, who in dedicating his young life, had intended to go into full-time medical service for God, was assigned as a medic to the army of occupation in Korea. Ironically, that's where I had dreamed of going as a child. Giles was sent to Texas with heavy artillery and became a noncommissioned officer in the tank corps.

As we watched the war clouds begin to billow over Vietnam, we waited anxiously upon the Lord and met the mailman halfway down the driveway each day. Those were long, hard, trying years.

It was good to have the babies and their parents to occupy our time and concern. Ten small lives now depended on us for their every need. Those times from the early years of my marriage, when I spent hours hearing tank builders' problems, were paying off; now I listened to parents who needed someone to listen. Their hearts were open to receive the Word of God.

For help with daily child care I turned to our local newspaper. The daughter of Dr. Sivon, a local physician, wrote an article asking for volunteers. We were not deluged with offers in response. However, Orpha Stoltzfus and Louella Schrock, two gracious Mennonite grandparents who lived nearby, came to mend, iron, and make clothes for our ever-changing family. This was not really what we had hoped for. We needed people who would assist with direct child care and perhaps even some who would help financially. We were desperate for funds.

Although we did not realize it at the time, those two humble women were the beginning of a widening circle of gentle, quiet persons who eventually made all the clothing and linens for hundreds of children who passed through our doors, pausing to rock the babies and bestow a kiss when they tired of sewing. They came from Youngstown, Hartville, Parkman, Aurora, Sugar Creek—Mennonites, Beachy Amish, Old Order Amish—wherever a settlement of plain people was to be found.

It was they, too, who would establish the Prayer and Faith Chapter of the Women's Auxiliary, our spiritual lifeline, throughout the coming years. Orpha's husband, Elmer, the bishop of the Aurora Plainview Mennonite Church, would become an important force on our trustee board and eventually acquaint us with the program of Mennonite Volunteer Service workers. We would have our child care workers eventually, all in God's good time.

No, we were not deluged with response at once, but God knew exactly whom we needed, and in his faithfulness sent the right people at the right time. We tried to remember the need to function within the framework of his timetable. It would be a while before our prayers were answered for direct financial help.

Society knew little or nothing about the problems faced by parents of these special children. Such children had too

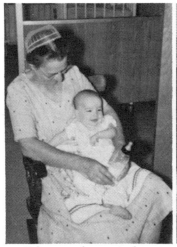

Volunteers often stopped to rock the babies.

God sent the right people to help us at the right time.

We accepted only babies who needed professional help and could not be cared for at home.

We needed people who would assist with direct child care and perhaps even financially.

often been hidden in attics and dark basements. Ours were the faceless children of the world.

After that first newspaper article we were frequently contacted by curiosity seekers, persons who called to ask the fee for seeing this kind of monstrosity or that. Our babies were not on display. This was not a zoo. There were so many problems to be overcome, so many giants lurking in dark corners.

We came face to face with one of those when Ginny came to live with us, soon after my boys went away. At age four, Ginny was only eighteen inches tall. She had survived many fractures. Her grandfather was a minister, her mother a Sunday school teacher. Her father, a professional man, was an expert in his field of work. Yet this family had no understanding of the needs of their little girl. When asked what she ate, Ginny's mother said, "Spaghetti, when her daddy comes home. She doesn't like me, you see." I was shocked.

"What about her formula?" I asked quickly, almost afraid to hear the answer.

"Why, I never thought to give her a drink," the mother said blankly. "Maybe that's why her tongue swells up and sticks out of her mouth," she added with a shrug.

"Doesn't she cry?" I asked, "and doesn't it bother you terribly?"

"I never hear her," she replied. "You see, she lives alone in the third-floor attic."

I couldn't believe what I was hearing. "Don't you hear her in your heart?" I asked.

This preliminary conversation was the first step down a long trail together for that mother and me. We spent many hours talking, with the woman growing more remorseful daily, as she came to realize what she had done.

Plans began to take shape. Together we decided to try through legislative action to prevent helpless children from suffering unnecessarily. Only a deeply sorrowing parent could have the stamina to join me for the long fight ahead.

We worked together with other parents who had joined forces under the banner of the powerful State Association known as OARC, the Ohio Association for Retarded Citizens. We joined The Legislative and Mercy Committees, which were destined to do so much to release our forgotten children—and older citizens as well—from the bondage and regimentation they had suffered so long. The human warehouses with all their horror stories would soon open their doors to reveal the hidden purgatory to an awakened public. Our deprived little Ginny was one of the cogs on the wheel that set a powerful dynamo in motion.

Our next visitor to the ever-crowded farmhouse was Chrit-Chee.

Perhaps the sound of the name related to her elfin qualities. Giles, who as a small boy had believed in elves, was fully convinced that Chrit-Chee belonged to that world of small industrious people—elves and leprechauns—who supposedly came to life at night.

Chrit-Chee was, however, a shy little French-Italian girl with a funny lopsided grin on a pointed face. Her drooping eyelids, her liquid black eyes, and the enormous mouth which spread her smile across the room, made her an adorable addition to the family. Sometimes even I, the realistic mother who didn't too much believe in elves, imagined her floating about the nurseries after dark, sprinkling stardust on all the sleeping babies.

In the daytime she curled up and hid her face under her arm with only one little pointed ear sticking up. Chrit-Chee, who didn't understand our language, nevertheless loved people. She spoke whole volumes with her dark little square hand, when it reached up timidly to pat my cheek.

In infancy Chrit-Chee was diagnosed as a totally deaf

"gargoyle." That is the medical term for ugly dwarf. We disagreed. She was beautiful. But her prognosis was not good, medically speaking. The doctors said she would never develop mentally or physically, because her body chemistry made it impossible for her to assimilate food properly.

I was not ready to admit defeat. I hoped and prayed that she would not be badly retarded, or really small. The hope was well founded.

For four years she grew considerably and gained weight to keep pace with her growth. Her powers of observation were remarkable. She was a persevering little person, and she put forth every effort to achieve the maximum of her capacity.

Still the notion never left us that some moonlit night Chrit-Chee would go sliding out on a moonbeam, never to be seen again. One night it happened. As she slept, Chrit-Chee drifted up to be with God. She had been loaned to us only for a little while.

We were learning that statistically the mortality rate for our special children would be high, even with the best of care. We could, however, bring comfort and happiness during the short span of their lives and, equally important, peace for the parents.

5
Ambitious Plans

> This is one of those cases in which the imagination is baffled by the facts.
>
> *Sir Winston Churchill*
> May 13, 1941
> Remark in the House of
> Commons following the
> parachute descent of
> Rudolph Hess in Scotland

It was about this time that Pat and Ann, two local housewives, began coming every Tuesday with a porta-crib covered with netting. With their help, we took the children onto the lawn as often as weather permitted. God had something special in mind for Pat and Ann. They themselves wouldn't forever be bathing and feeding our precious children.

One day when the heat was suffocating and our babies were irritable from the temperature, Ann wiped her brow and said, "Surely there is a better way than this."

"Do you know any millionaires?" I joked.

"Yes, I do," she replied. "My husband!"

I had not suspected that the charming housewife who came so faithfully from Aurora each week with her friend was from a family of great wealth and prominence in her community. Her friend also revealed herself to be equally affluent—in fact, she was a member of the DuPont family!

The conversation that followed was astounding as they discussed which of their acquaintances would be interested in advancing enough money to develop a truly adequate facility for the children. Ann said, "This isn't the kind of thing George would do."

"Or Bob," Pat agreed. "But how about Ned Sargent?"

As for me, I was still in shock when Ned arrived that same evening, bending his six-foot-six frame to get through our door. Ned was president of a chemical firm, Zirconium Corporation of America. He towered over the cribs peering intently into the faces of our dear children. He left silently, but God had spoken to his heart. We would hear from him again. He was not only a physical and mental giant; his heart was just as big as his frame.

It was Ned Sargent who organized a board of directors. He introduced us to his banker, Rudolph Garfield, from National City Bank of Cleveland and to his corporation's attorney, Ed Crane, who would later write the constitution for our corporation.

To me it seemed that Ned was able to open magic doors where untold treasures lay waiting to be used for the babies that he too had grown to love. His was a vision of growth and development in facilities that would become known worldwide. The lives of thousands would be enriched through his concern for those he called "the least of God's dear children."

Ned Sargent was clay in the hands of God. God was shaping him into a vessel designed to serve the needs of profoundly dysfunctional infants and their families. Through his contact with our helpless children he would come to know God in a more personal way. Ned's energies never flagged. His zeal never waned. His was the enthusiasm that renewed each of us when our courage faltered. "Where there is no vision, the people perish," we read in Proverbs 29:18. Ned's was a great vision. He didn't intend to see any of these special children perish, if there was a way to prevent it. There would be discouragements and dark nights; but with Ned's vision we could go on, hand in hand with God.

A new canticle was born in our hearts.

> Through the night, lest I fall,
> Guide my steps, to your call.
> Take my hand, precious Lord
> . . . lest I fall.

God opened other doors with equally startling results.

About this time a young certified public accountant and his wife came to our door, seeking placement for their infant son, who had been born with profound problems. It was no simple decision for us to make. Young David's condition required more technical and medical attention than any of our other current little boarders. He required an iron lung.

When we agreed to make room for David, we knew we were entering a new medical arena. We had no idea, however, that we were also entering a new financial arena!

When we finally agreed to accept David, his father asked in wonder, "Don't you know we are Jews?" I had not considered the family's religion or nationality. It would have made no difference if I had. Long ago I had learned that neither creed, color, nor race made any difference, when my brother married one of the sweetest, most gentle girls in the world. Leona, my sister-in-law, was the daughter of our best neighbor, a family of Crow Indians.

Now these warm young Jewish parents opened their

hearts to us and began bringing into our lives a whole new circle of wealthy and influential Jewish friends—the Rosenbaums, Klines, Cohens, Applebaums, Epsteins, and many other fine people who joined our ranks and worked to secure funding resources. They were also our source of encouragement to incorporate the work officially.

Dick, meanwhile, had spoken to his union officials about the work we were doing. The business agent for Operating Engineers Local 18 was Frank Converse, a tough individual who had come up through the ranks during the days when it was kick-and-scratch all the way. His name was a legend in the ranks of labor. Perhaps it was because Frank Converse knew what it meant to be in difficult circumstances that he sympathized with our children and their parents. Under his leadership the first endowment fund was established for our

There was much to receive as well as to give.

foundation—a fund which would provide a crib for the child of any union member who might have the misfortune to need our services for one of his children. God is merciful and loving, rewarding those who express love. In 17 years of existence, that fund has never been needed for an operator's child.

Our reward has been great also. Of the $200,000 that came into the fund, much was eventually approved for use in the expansion of our facilities. This in turn has blessed dozens of families whose infants have lived—and also died—in the comfortable new wing, made possible in part by this endowment.

The Operating Engineers' wives, not to be outdone, organized auxiliary chapters, some as far away as Springfield, Ohio, and annually brought in truckloads of supplies at Christmas. We were learning to believe God, as his blessings poured in.

During the second summer, we began to talk—rather desperately—of construction. The old farmhouse was bulging with babies and the people who cared for them.

By the spring of 1963 we had eleven babies (although our license limited us to ten), over 100 applicants were waiting for admission, laundry facilities were inadequate, and winter would bring real hardships. Our situation was desperate— sometimes excruciatingly so.

Of the dozens of applicants we were forced to reject because of limited space, one stands foremost in my mind. The family ran out of money to pay the hospital bill, just as Alice's parents had. When they brought the baby home there was no money for oxygen, and she died. The horrified mother then shot and killed herself.

She was a close neighbor. Like so many others she had begged us to take "just one more baby." Three healthy children and a bewildered husband were left mourning the

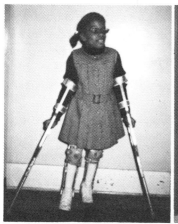

We would not discharge any child until suitable accommodations could be found elsewhere.

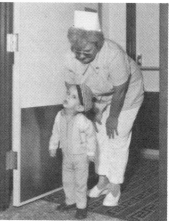

"Trisome 21" amazed the staff by surviving, and then by going home and entering public school.

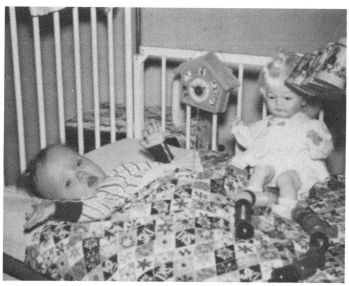

The surroundings for dozens of the children have been brightened with funds from the operating engineers.

loss of this wife and mother. Surely someone, somewhere had some responsibility to this family.

Had we taken that one extra child, we would have lost our license. I could find no fault with that regulation because I had seen the dreadful overcrowded state facilities and knew there was good reason to draw a firm line somewhere. We were convinced, however, that once again something had to be done.

Dick, Ned, and I put our heads together to plan proper housing. The timing was right; God's timing is always right.

We found that President Kennedy had approved legislation to provide funds for development of private facilities for citizens of any age, who required supervised living accommodations. This was largely due to the fact that his family had experienced great difficulty in securing adequate service for his mentally retarded sister. He had learned firsthand about the inadequacy of housing, as well as inhumane treatment and the lack of medical care and training and educational opportunities. We were on the brink of a tremendous revolution in planning for retarded citizen care. Soon we would be hearing a great deal about "the rights of the retarded."

We felt reasonably sure our operation would qualify for some of that federal assistance if we incorporated.

Ed Crane, Ned's corporate attorney, arranged to incorporate our work as "The Hattie Larlham Foundation, Inc." (This was Dick's choice of name for our proposed nonprofit corporation.)

PURPOSE, for which The Hattie Larlham Foundation, Inc., was formed:

1. To establish, maintain and operate an institution for physically, neurologically or otherwise damaged children; to provide custodial care for such children; to provide medical care

and treatment for the advancement of such children toward normalcy, and to engage in research work of a preventative and therapeutic nature with relation to such persons; to charge and receive compensation for treatment, services and accommodations; all for the purpose of maintaining such institution and doing any and all things necessary or incidental thereto.

2. To acquire or receive from any persons, firms, associations, or corporations by deed, gift, purchase, bequest, devise, or otherwise, cash, securities, and other property, tangible and intangible, real and personal, and to hold, administer, manage, invest and to reinvest, and to disburse the principal and income thereof for the purpose hereof; and

3. To purchase, acquire, hold, convey, lease, mortgage or dispose of property, real or personal, tangible or intangible, and to do such other things as may be necessary or advisable directly or indirectly to effectuate the foregoing purposes.

My husband Dick, our son Charles, and I were named incorporators. We subsequently compiled a board of trustees from among our closest and most faithful supporters.

That board was made up of Frank Converse, our labor representative; Elmer Stoltzfus, the local Mennonite pastor (whom Ned later characterized as "the most astute man I've ever known"); Sheldon Epstein, C.P.A.; Rudolph Garfield, banker; Ed Crane, attorney; Earl Mizer, local financier; Ned Sargent, industrialist; and Dick, Charles, and me. I felt we also needed a physician in the group. I didn't know whom to ask, but God led me to him in an unusual way.

I had been diligently sketching floor plans to turn over to an architect. One day while in Cleveland, carrying the sketches in my car, I ran into a sudden summer storm that deluged the road. Since I could go no farther, I stopped my car at a medical center (as I later realized) and rushed into the lobby. It was empty except for the receptionist, and we fell into conversation. Before long I had told her my dream of a functionally designed facility for my dear children.

"Let me introduce you to Dr. John Allen," she said.

God had led me through the storm to the physician for our board of trustees. Dr. Allen, a member of the Neurological Board of Ohio, was director of the Comprehensive Care Center for disabled children at Metropolitan General Hospital in Cleveland. They were doing extensive research on mental retardation, prevention, habilitation, and treatment. Dr. Allen had established an outreach for extended care at Health Hill in Cleveland and was currently looking for just such a facility as the one we were planning to build. That very day he committed himself to our cause.

We registered with the state of Ohio as a nonprofit corporation. Our statement of philosophy reflected our belief in the value and sanctity of life, regardless of the apparent lack of ability to function in a productive manner in society.

This was truly revolutionary thinking! Until this time, government agencies at every level had been willing to subsidize care only for human beings who had the potential to become productive citizens. The ten board members whom God had brought together formulated a code of regulations and proceeded to solicit funds to erect a facility that would accommodate fifty "non-salvageable," nonambulatory infants, requiring long-term residential services.

We announced that we would accept only those babies who needed professional expertise and could not be cared for at their own homes. We would not accept a child over six years of age. According to the laws of Ohio, the State Department of Mental Health and Mental Retardation was responsible only for the care of those six years of age and over, who were mentally retarded. However, we would not discharge any child from our facility until suitable accommodations could be found elsewhere, even if they had passed the age of six years.

Preparation for the big step went forward, powered by

prayer with fasting and much hard work. In addition to caring for the children now in our home, there were architectural plans to complete and calls to make in the hope of raising funds from our friends, acquaintances, and local business people. Members of my family also began to rally round, each helping according to the gifts God had given them. Those years of early childhood training would weld us together to perform a mighty work for God.

It was disappointing to find that most of the people we contacted wanted to see bricks and mortar before they contributed. The federal funds were not yet available.

In the meantime, I was working far into the night on floor plans. I knew no better way than to buy a copy of the Ohio building code, study it diligently, and draw my plans accordingly. An expert would have called it madness. Today I might too, except for the fact that we could not afford architectural fees and I knew I must depend on God to guide my hand. We had no money, none whatsoever. The banks were of course unwilling to risk a loan until we had substantial support. The restricting circle was tight; *no support would be forthcoming until we had funds; no funds were available until we had support.* We were at an impasse.

The tide turned in November when Dick attended the annual statewide meeting of operating engineers, held in Columbus, Ohio, our capital city. There he spoke to ten thousand operators from all over Ohio about the needs of our "Dear Children." God blessed his words. Before he finished speaking, a line had formed. As those men dropped their bills on the podium, the money gradually overflowed the speaker's stand and began to spread across the floor.

We knew God had spoken to hearts in answer to prayer. We were on our way.

The very next day, Rudy (Bob) Garfield called to ask if I would meet with his friends from the Leonard C. Hanna

Fund in Cleveland and tell them of our needs.

When I went to prayer meeting that night and asked God's people to pray that we might be worthy of the commission being laid upon us, I felt we would receive the necessary help if we were still planning according to his will.

The next day Rudy and I walked into a conference room where forty of Cleveland's financial magnates periodically met to set policy for the foundations of Cleveland to use as guidelines in making their decisions about contributions. Mr. Wolf was presiding at the head of the conference table, which looked to me like the longest table in the world. These were the friends Rudy had spoken of. Mr. Wolf introduced me to the group and said, "Now tell us what it is you need."

In that moment I felt all of the insecurities of that little mountain girl I had been long ago in the hills of West Virginia. But God was with us in that conference room. As I talked, a great quiet settled upon the multimillionaires seated around the table. I was able to speak simply of the needs of our children.

"And how much do you need?" Rudy's friend Mr. Wolf asked.

"Ask largely," an inner voice prompted.

"Dear God," I thought in that split second, "what does largely mean?"

"Ten thousand dollars," I told them.

"And when do you need this money?"

"Yesterday," I replied quickly.

"Write the lady a check," Mr. Wolf directed. Rudy and I left in a state of euphoria. God had shown us that all things are possible when he is in control. I remembered again that the cattle on a thousand hills are his (Psalm 50:10).

While we had both been busy raising funds, Dick had pushed ahead in another area. He had found a licensed engineer who put my plans on blueprint paper and affixed his seal at no charge. We were now ready to go back to the bank with a detailed funding proposal.

Mr. Mizer, president of the local bank, was also the treasurer of our board of trustees. There was no difficulty when he presented our proposal to the officers of the bank. We now had good backing and a sound plan of action.

Dick and I would personally give thirty acres of our farm, valued at $1,000 per acre, to the foundation. Thus the total amount of cash already raised was well over $50,000. Would the bank give us a letter approving a loan of $50,000?

Yes, they would!

We were over the first big hurdle.

My sisters were terribly concerned about the risk, but every one of them rallied to the cause. Even my aged, ailing mother made bed pads, sitting in the nursery in her wheelchair. She adored our babies.

Like all the rest of us, Mom had her favorite. She spent many hours rocking and singing her old ballads to Grandmaw Tippy-Toe, who weighed just two pounds at the age of six months. Grandmaw Tippy-Toe was small enough that even Mom, frail as she was, did not tire of holding her.

Tippy-Toe occupied a strange and unusual little body, with silk-like wavy black hair falling over her shoulders and a tiny wizened face accented by a hooked nose. Her little pointed ears lay flat against her head, projecting far up along the temples. Her nickname came from our imaginations. To us this baby, like Chrit-Chee before her, seemed elf-like. It was a sad day for my mother when Grandmaw Tippy-Toe quietly ceased to breathe. Her pea-sized brain was too small to sustain life as she grew older.

My sister Ella and her husband, Bill, now a carpenter, were among our chief supporters. Bill went with me to the state capitol in Columbus, to present our plans. His trade had taught him how tough the Department of Building and Factory Inspection could be.

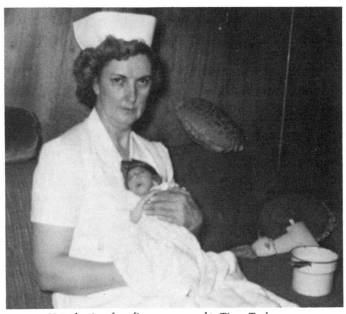

Note the size of my fingers compared to Tippy-Toe's arm.

Having driven 200 miles, we were on the steps of the government building on Front Street at 5:00 a.m., waiting for the doors to open at 7:00 a.m. Even so, there were several people ahead of us. We waited anxiously all day, watching those ahead of us leaving in defeat one by one—bearing long lists of recommendations for corrections on their blueprints. I grew more and more apprehensive, with misgivings about the plans I had drawn. In my mind I tried to remember frost depth, stress and strain, load-bearing requirements, and countless other technical data I hoped I wouldn't be asked to justify.

As the day dragged on, I felt sure our plans wouldn't be approved. I was afraid to go out to lunch lest we be called and I miss my turn. Satan had used this day to bring discouragement, and he would try to top it off with defeat if he possibly could—which seemed inevitable. Every bit of confidence I had acquired vanished during that awful day. I could identify with Elijah when he sat under the juniper tree in fear of Jezabel and wanted to die (1 Kings 19:3-4).

At 5:30 p.m. Zoyd Flaler, the chief engineer with the department, came out to tell us we would have to return the following day. We weren't prepared to stay overnight. I begged him to look at our plans briefly, at least, since we had traveled so far. Mr. Flaler finally agreed to give us just fifteen minutes.

I scarcely breathed as he pored intently over our blueprints, one page after another. Finally he put his red pencil to the paper—but there was only one minor correction. The error was in a stairway drawing, and that was all! The plans were approved with no design changes! All the basics of our structure were sound as planned.

Only God's hand guiding mine could have achieved this miracle. "Not my will but yours, God," I vowed that evening.

We arrived home at 11:00 p.m. to cold corned beef and cabbage, thoughtfully left out by Lyndella. I took no time to heat it, but ate quickly and tumbled into bed. I had been up for forty-two hours.

The anxiety and subsequent rebound had taken their toll, and Satan would not lose quietly.

6
Facilities for Fifty

Although human life is priceless, we always act as if something had an even greater price than life. . . . But what is that something?

Antoine de Saint-Exupery
Vol de Nuit

Sometime during the night following our day of victory in Columbus, I awakened with terrible cramps and nausea. I managed to find a bucket and set it beside the bed. Exhausted, I fell asleep again only to waken periodically, lean over the bucket, and fall back in a stupor. After a time there was no longer strength or inclination to lean over the bucket. When my daughter Lyndella came to say goodbye before leaving for school, she found blood in the bucket and splattered over the bed, and an unconscious mother.

I was rushed to the hospital by ambulance. Later I learned that a massive ulcer had perforated my stomach. The hemorrhaging would surely have killed me if Lyndella had not come to say goodbye.

Later, when transfusions and a stomach suction machine

had done their reviving work, Dr. Knowlton talked about surgery. The pancreas was undoubtedly damaged as well, he said, and might give me permanent problems. But in my spirit I felt a deep resolve. The encounter over the blueprints in Columbus had confirmed for me that God had a purpose in my life and Satan could not defeat it.

As I rededicated my life to God, his healing love flooded my body. Dr. Knowlton scoffed at my attitude and kept me in the hospital for three weeks under rigid treatment. When I went home laden with medications, a diet, and complicated instructions, I promised my troubled medical friend that I would stay both with his plan of treatment and with my faith in God for six months, and then he could talk about operating again if he still found it necessary. He insisted that an ulcer the size of mine, especially with the pancreas eroded, could not be healed by any medical treatment available. I knew that God had already healed me—totally. I promised to not overtax my body again.

I had forgotten that this body was the temple of God. I would need to remember that Christ loved that temple and expected me to care for it responsibly. I would do this for his sake.

The ulcer disappeared. Neither X-ray nor any other method of medical investigation ever found it again. I was healed, and the doctors could not explain what had happened.

Those three weeks alone in the hospital, away from the stress of daily living and the burden of child care, gave me time for assessment. Any doubts of direction were gone. I went home fully committed to our task. That old debt for my ticket to Joppa had finally been paid in full, and I was on my way to do God's bidding at last.

By fall, Dick had convinced one of his contractor buddies, Miles Friend, to start the construction job immediately.

Since I had written no specifications, Miles would write them as the job progressed, using donated labor and materials as they came to hand. Truly, this first building was constructed with faith and love. Miles had faith in us; we had faith in God.

My sister Edna, who lived with Mom and cared for her, took a part of each day to solicit funds. She went from store to store, accumulating pledges for furnishings and equipment.

She and Pat (one of those first wealthy volunteers) put together the women's auxiliary for our foundation with chapters in surrounding villages and cities. (Ultimately, the auxiliary spread throughout the state, with hundreds of supporters, rich and poor, unsaved and Christian alike—all women working together for the love of humanity.

Edna's husband, Orville, now an upholsterer with a local firm, started making foam rubber mattresses covered with red hospital rubber. We used those for many years, along with little upholstered chairs and other special supports fashioned by his competent hands for the children he too had grown to love.

Winnie and her husband, Phil Hayden, assembled 30 slides he had taken—pictures of our lovely helpless babies. Winnie and Phil shared information about our special ministry to groups of worshipers of nearly every denomination, and later to civic organizations, women's clubs, and union halls.

As all kinds of organizations responded to Winnie and Phil's presentation with gifts, a volunteer service organization began to develop. Gertrude came to work as a volunteer typist and switchboard operator. None of this, however, was as great as the prayer cells they established.

Winnie and Phil also later organized the Ways and Means Committee, which developed dinners, bazaars, flea markets,

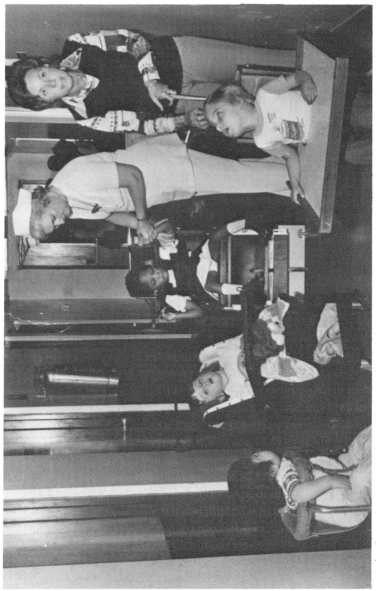

My brother-in-law Orville fashioned little upholstered chairs and other special supports for the children he too had grown to love.

rummage sales, hospitality gift shops, and numerous other fund-raising projects. Down through the years no one has been more instrumental in doing fund-raising or been better at public relations than those wonderful people—dedicated members of my family and, indeed, of the family of God.

Edna developed a series of stations for trading stamp deposits and ran a series of articles in the local newspapers calling attention to them. This resource alone brought in over $30,000 a year, while providing a way for retirees to become involved in a worthy activity. The early years of faithful Christian training were bringing in dividends for God. That long shadow of my father's faithful ministry to his family was lengthening out.

Again Dick went to the union. Through that contact, Standard Slag and Gravel of Youngstown, Ohio, gave the sand and gravel and all of the windows for our new building. The Operating Engineers Union did the grading, moving hundreds of yards of dirt in one day. It seemed impossible that so many kinds of heavy machinery and so many operators could be organized to work efficiently on one site at one time, but they were. Glaziers from Akron put in the windows. Our Mennonite neighbors, excellent craftsmen, built the cabinetry and painted the woodwork. Flexicore and cement blocks came at greatly reduced rates from sympathetic manufacturers. A Rotary club from Geauga County painted all the inside walls. Suddenly we had become news, and it seemed as though people vied with each other to see who could do the most. Finally the building was completed. Like the wall around Jerusalem built by Nehemiah, it was God's cause and everyone had a mind to work (Nehemiah 4:6).

A reporter from Channel 8 in Cleveland came out to see what was happening. Later he returned with a mobile production team to follow us through an entire day of work with the children and with the supervision of our construc-

The Operating Engineers Union did the grading, moving hundreds of yards of dirt in one day.

tion. The series presented by Ted Wygant brought publicity to our work in many areas where we would never have been able to gain recognition otherwise.

Open house in April of 1964 was almost three years after our first little Alice had come to live with us. By that day, God had brought together dozens of dissimilar personalities for a singular and unique cause.

Open house would have been complete for me if the boys could have come home for the event. Chuck was still in Korea and Giles in Texas. Giles had married; he and Kathy were expecting a new member in their own family at any moment.

At 10:00 a.m. on April 25, just as Mr. Wolf came to our door, the telephone rang. Giles announced the birth of our first grandchild, Michael Ryerson Larlham—a perfect baby. For awhile I almost forgot about the dignitaries and open house and all of the rest of it. What beauty there was in God's grace that day!

The war in Vietnam, however, was heating up—another mental burden. Either son could be called up at any time. What would my boys be like when they came home? Would they come home? Would there be a future for young Mike? In those days I felt unusually close to our handicapped babies—perhaps because their futures were more assured in many ways than that of our own sons. They were warm, well fed, clothed, loved, secure. Perhaps theirs, after all, was the better life.

I finally settled back to the matter of open house. Present that day were my husband and myself as well as my sisters and their husbands and children. And there were Elmer and Orpha Stoltzfus, our dearest friends and constant counselors, as close to us as parents. There were the Amish farmers and craftsmen and their families who had worked side by side with folks of other customs and religions. Like the Recabites

Dick and I were grateful to God and to the many friends who had cooperated to turn our dream into reality.

of old, they continued to abide by the dictates of their faith (Jeremiah 35).

There were the representatives of various construction trades; our local business people who had contributed products and services; elite women from wealthy residential areas, who served refreshments, wives of physicians from swanky Twin Lakes, and of industrialists from upper-class Solon and Aurora, as well as wives of Jewish professionals and merchants from Shaker Heights.

The operating engineers and major contractors came wearing their hard hats in memory of the groundbreaking day, months before, when those tons of earth had been moved by loaned machinery and donated labor from Akron and Cleveland.

Miles, our faithful contractor, was pleased that he had been able to mold everything into a facility, strong and somehow beautiful, but a little embarrassed at the praises heaped upon him.

Our guests also included Pastor Walter Banks and his beautiful black choir of Negro voices from the Bible Baptist Church of Warrensville—wonderful friends we will cherish forever.

Jews, Gentiles, Catholics, and Protestants participated—people of a half-dozen races, rich and poor, polished professionals and dirt farmers, parents and children. All joined together in their common bond of love for God's dear little "unsalvageable" children.

Rabbi Rosenthal brought the invocation and Judge Summers delivered an address. Pastor Elmer Stoltzfus dedicated the building. Ironically, no dignitaries from the Department of Mental Health and Mental Retardation were in our audience. Instead, the people around us were our neighbors and friends and people God had brought into our lives through association with the babies. We congratulated each other as babies were moved into their new quarters.

We now had facilities for fifty children. A building worth much more had been erected for only $100,000 because "the people had a mind to work." We had followed God's perfect timetable.

For two hundred years our government and its agencies had closed their eyes to the needs of citizens who couldn't quite cope with life. Hundreds of thousands of children down through those many decades had been pushed into dismal, overcrowded barracks-like facilities, or shut into bedroom closets and attics. There they had been underfed, neglected, abused, or left to fend off the more aggressive people in their environment as best they could. Most domestic animals had fared much better.

Although rights for the retarded was an important new concept, the doors of our facility opened for the first time to only a handful of reporters, other than those from the local newspapers.

Public funding for our little charges was still not available because the law contained no provision for financing the care of mentally retarded persons under six years of age. The Ohio Division of Mental Health and Mental Retardation was even reluctant to license us. Welfare children's service boards could not buy our services because of the language of the law, which reserved those funds for battered and neglected children. Most of our children were not in that category. Who would batter so helpless an infant? One father had been told that he would receive funds to have his child cared for if he left her on the street—but he would find himself in jail.

Finally, Dr. Wayne Chess, director of Mental Health and Mental Retardation, licensed The Hattie Larlham Foundation, Inc., as a specialized treatment center. It was new language, undefined but certainly suitable to our purpose.

There were still no public funds available for operational expense. It soon became evident we would need to continue fund raising because the parents most in need of our assistance were least likely to be able to meet even our modest fees of $175 a month per child. The state officials were amazed that we could provide professional care at a per diem rate under six dollars when it was costing well over $20 in state facilities for custodial care.

Our care included, as needed for each child, medication, oxygen, resuscitation, special diets, incubation, intubation for blended feedings, rotating physicians on call, and dozens of other special medical services. It was essential to have a registered nurse on duty 24 hours a day. Somewhere the funds must be found to maintain this level of care. In the meantime, the medical staff agreed that we should limit our admissions to no more than two babies a week and concentrate on developing a personalized, structured program for each new arrival. With the backlog of applications, decisions concerning priority of placement acceptance were difficult to make. We determined not to be influenced by the financial status of any family after being offered $10,000 by parents if we would accept their mongoloid child. The most crucial determining factor had to be the need of the child weighed against the parents' lack of ability to meet that need, and the need within the family to find respite from the overwhelming stress within that family.

Before long our women's auxiliary decided to take action. A diligent search of the Ohio code had revealed a statute that mandated legislative action be taken if a specific petition bearing 200,000 signatures was presented to the governor. We drafted our petition carefully, with legal assistance, to make sure the language was right. It called for

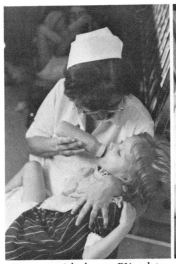

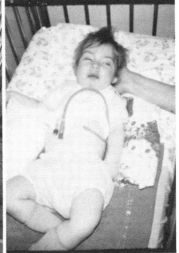

It was essential to have an RN on duty 24 hours a day.

Our care was tailored to the special needs of each child.

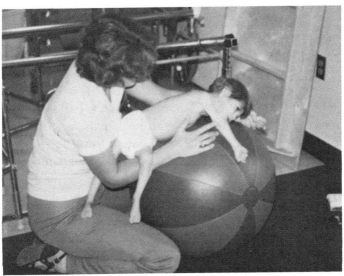

We developed a personalized, structured program for each new arrival.

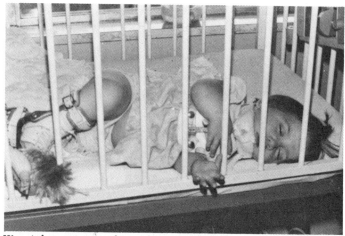
We tried to point out the wisdom of early intervention to develop latent potential and avoid institutionalization at a later age.

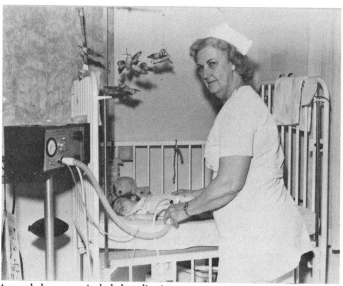
As needed, our care included medication, oxygen, resuscitation, special diets, incubation, intubation for blended feedings, rotating physicians on call, and dozens of other special services.

the state of Ohio to guarantee retarded children from birth through six years of age the same right to residential care, treatment, and training services and funding reimbursement as those of school age or older. The auxiliary members sent copies of the petition to their chapter chairmen across the state with the goal of acquiring the required number of signatures.

In the meantime Mr. Larlham and I sought out Ohio legislators with empathy for our cause. We had been working actively with the Legislative Committee of the Ohio Association for Retarded Citizens and had become well acquainted with our local congressmen. Mark Roberto (Ravenna), Troy Lee James (Cleveland), and Bill Batchelder (Medina) together developed House Bill 549 for presentation to committee. We knew we would have the powerful support of OARC behind us.

The skirmishes began immediately. The Commissioner of Mental Retardation opposed our philosophy, arguing that babies like ours needed a one-to-one relationship with their parents. He questioned whether I was "an angel with a halo or a witch on a broom." By this time I was a familiar figure in committee rooms and legislative halls, as well as in the office of the commissioner. We knew that in a sense he was right. Some parents are able to cope reasonably well with their severely handicapped child. But our clients had problems too big to cope with in a family setting. Neither were we campaigning for admission to state facilities. Actually, we were stressing the need for early diagnostic evaluation followed by specialized treatment and training which could be handled only in a residential setting, with adequate staffing. As for me, I was simply a compassionate woman wanting to bring comfort to the children and hope to their families. We tried to point out to the commissioner the wisdom of early intervention to develop latent potential and

We presented a petition with 200,000 signatures to Ohio Governor John Gilligan. It asked the state to guarantee retarded children from birth through six years of age the same right to residential care, treatment, and training services and funding reimbursement as those of school age or older.

thus avoid institutionalization at a later age. We had not yet developed statistics to support that kind of claim and were unable to convince this man who had spent many years of frustration monitoring state facilities.

He continually referred to the limitations of the "warehouses" already in operation for human beings. He argued that there would never be enough money to adequately care for those to whom the state was already committed. He had absolutely no intention of complicating things and making matters worse by adding an infant population to his already overloaded and understaffed facilities. Furthermore, he was not prepared to undertake the gigantic

94

struggle necessary to change the system. From my perspective, here was a defeated man without a vision. This was bureaucracy at its worst.

Ohio was fortunate at that time to have as governor John Gilligan, a man sympathetic to the needs of the masses— even though that very sympathy would eventually lead to his losing the next election.

Governor Gilligan was repelled by those who pointed out that the mentally retarded had no vote. He was a champion of those people whose needs were greatest.

In less than a year my husband and I were ready to approach the governor with that enormous roll of signatures our auxiliary women had been preparing. The news media were also ready to give us coverage because something sensational was going on. Radio, television, and newspaper reporters covered the story as the governor accepted the huge roll of petitions and signatures carried on a pole between Dick and me. Cameras flashed and reporters scurried about as we climbed the long flight of steps on State Street to enter the great rotunda of the capitol building. The governor was waiting for us, surrounded by enlarged pictures of our children which had been placed on easels all around the wall. At the ceremony that followed, Governor Gilligan went on public record as a supporter of our position.

The news went out all across Ohio. Our babies had found a real champion. The bill never got out of committee. It wasn't necessary. We were called back to Columbus the next week by State Representative and Finance Committee Chairman Myrl H. Schumacher, and the commissioner. They advised us that official action had already been taken to change the department's policy. An executive order, with the full force of legislative action, had already been put into effect. The state house had been deluged with angry letters during the previous week. The governor had learned of the

Our children were now eligible for the same services as other retarded citizens in Ohio, a real victory for parents.

plight of thousands of developmentally disabled children throughout the country—more than 2,000 in Ohio alone. The Ohio Commissioner of Mental Retardation had no choice but to capitulate. The bill would be unnecessary. Indeed, it would take too long. The governor's mandate was God's answer to the needs of his "Dear Children."

Now age would be no barrier to service. Our children were eligible for the same services as other retarded citizens in Ohio which, although insufficient, was a real victory for parents. The OARC joined hands with our enthusiastic auxiliary workers. We were to be co-workers for many years to come in securing needed legislation and funding resources to assure humane treatment for retarded persons. A great step forward had been taken.

Before the holidays, Dick and I were invited to the annual award dinner held in the governor's mansion. There we received the Ohio Certificate of Recognition for the most significant contribution to mankind. If we had coveted political recognition, we might well have felt we had reached the pinnacle. We were indeed grateful to God and the governor for doors that would open because of the public recognition of need for assistance to the parents of our precious children. We were humble before God because he had entrusted us with this great commission.

Ours was not the only country where the very young had been overlooked. Dick and I had attended the fourth World Conference on Mental Retardation, held in Boston, Massachusetts, where we learned from representatives of 42 countries that nowhere in the world was there adequate assistance for parents who had the misfortune to give birth to a profoundly dysfunctional baby.

7
New Programs and Techniques

Don't look back. Something may be gaining on you.

Leroy Paige
How to Keep Young

Our hard-won "equal rights" really meant little. The big job ahead was to obtain for all of our retarded citizens the same rights as those of every normal citizen. Only then could we do a truly competent job of helping parents find appropriate placement for their handicapped babies all the way through the maze of treatment which included training, loving care, and in many cases habilitation.

Our organizational structure at the home base was developing nicely and becoming highly functional. Winnie and Phil were great fund raisers. Edna worked in the office three days a week writing letters of appeal and establishing a filing system. The women's auxiliary had thrived on their arduous commission; their many community activities had doubled their membership.

We were staffed with good and concientious clerical and

medical personnel, including a newly employed social worker. Beds were filling up rapidly. Within six months after completion of the building every crib was filled and we had another list of waiting applicants. We began to realize as never before that some of our "nonsalvageable" darlings had been classified wrongly. There were brilliant intellects trapped in malformed physical structures which could be corrected by surgery.

> Tho' sorrows befall us and Satan oppose,
> God leads his dear children along.
> Thro' grace we can conquer, defeat all
> our foes.
> God leads his dear children along.

"Dear God, we are so lacking in wisdom," I prayed. "You must surely lead us all the way."

There was Cindy, who had difficulty breathing because of a dreadful stridor in her throat. The two-year-old baby, with beautiful curly red hair, had never spoken a word. Little Cindy could no longer live at home because she had suffered so many bouts of pneumonia and required constant medical attention.

When she came to live with us she turned her face to the wall and avoided human contact whenever possible. Eventually she began making approaches to her rag doll. It was evident that she had been watching what was going on around her because we found her pretending to take its temperature, wash its face, and change its diaper.

One night when the lights were low and everyone was quiet except one crying baby, Cindy called out, "Give baby a beer!" We were amazed. No one had heard her utter a word before. Having broken her silence with that phrase, she talked up a storm, learning new words rapidly. Mrs. Mester, our social worker, began looking into Cindy's past case history and found the source of her problem. Cindy wasn't ill. Nor was she retarded. This poor child had been traumatized by her early environment. As she gained confidence and security, her symptoms disappeared.

How many of our babies, we began to wonder, had a future? Soon we began recording and maintaining those statistics I had wished for when contending with the commissioner. I sensed how rewarding it would be to find out how effective habilitation really was. There were so many unanswered questions, so much to be done. I prayed silently over and over, "Dear God, give me wisdom."

Little "Bill-Bill" lived for four years in a soundproof box in the attic of his grandparents' home; even the neighbors didn't know of his existence. His mother had died giving birth and his father had disappeared soon afterward. The grandparents did what seemed best to them for this strange little creature. Bill had been born with his legs permanently flexed outward at right angles from the hips and sharply inward at the knees. He had a strange, malformed little face with sparkling eyes. It was not hard to see the mischief that lurked there, but being non-vocal, he had no way of expressing it. The grandparents, who took him when his mother died, were told that he had been destroyed before birth by the radiation treatment given his mother for cancer she developed during pregnancy. Didn't his odd face and distorted limbs prove it? Eventually his grandmother could no longer cope with her own emotional problems, and Bill came to live with us.

Lyndella was home from college for summer vacation, having just completed her first year at Bluffton. She was working in our kitchen to supplement her fall tuition. She liked to put Bill in a wheelchair and take him to the kitchen with her, mostly because his eyes were so bright and inquisitive. Although he had never spoken a word, she was con-

As Cindy gained confidence and security, her symptoms disappeared.

Happiness is . . . returning home.

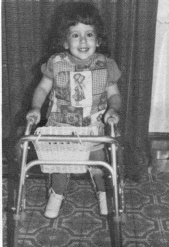

Because of early intervention for their hydrocephalic condition, Patrick (left) and Sarah (right) are able to live productive lives in their adoptive home.

vinced he surely could. One day while she made pies and chattered with Bill, she turned suddenly, jabbed him playfully with her doughy finger, and said, "Bill, you are a lemon!"

"You-le-mo," Bill responded.

Lyndella came racing into my office shouting, "He can talk! Bill can talk! Mom, Bill can talk!"

Talk he did, from that day on, nonstop, about everything that had been bottled up inside him. Even more fascinating was the fact that Bill didn't have to learn baby talk first. He hadn't missed much that went on around him after he got out of his box, and he picked up words at an incredible speed. They weren't always the best ones, but they were words, and he was learning to talk in well-formed sentences that made good sense. Soon he was tumbling out of his wheelchair, balancing himself on his hands, and learning to get around. Bill had a special crawl—sort of a scoot. He pulled himself along, hand over hand like a seal, with his crooked little legs following limply along behind. He developed powerful chest and shoulder muscles and eventually walked well on his hands with the rest of his body arched upward.

Eager to learn, he gave us all kinds of problems. He tried to climb into and onto everything. He crawled over the side of his crib to meet our guests at the door. He waddled up and down stairs, undaunted by his strange method of mobility. He even began trying to read from the few children's books we kept around for visitors. It was evident that Bill, a former nonsalvageable, had a brighter future than most of the children we had sheltered. The psychologist who had done a cursory evaluation earlier in Bill's life refused to see him again or refer him to anyone else for reevaluation. He had gone so far as to advise Crippled Children's Services that they should never underwrite any treatment for Bill.

It was time for God to take a hand. The Prayer and Faith Chapter of the women's auxiliary began to intercede for Bill. We went to Kent State University, only eight miles away, to emplore them to supply us with an evaluation. They complied, and Bill tested out as having the mental ability of a six-year-old. He had gleaned six years of knowledge in only six months. Dr. John Allen, the pediatric neurologist from Cleveland, our medical adviser on the trustee board, suggested Bill be taken to the comprehensive care center at Metropolitan General Hospital for corrective orthopedic surgery. My husband approached the Grand Master of the Shriners at the local lodge, telling him of our needs for funds to assure Bill of the opportunity to lead a normal life. The Shriners magnanimously agreed to underwrite all costs.

Little Bill was in Cleveland several months. Following extensive surgery on his hips, knees, and feet he went to Health Hill, an habilitation center, where he began learning to walk. At first, Bill resented being slowed down by his braced legs. He had made such rapid progress without those braces. Even before he could walk well, they had him in school. There was no stopping him. He might not yet be running in his braces but he was running ahead in educational progress. Bill, it turned out, had an unusually high IQ.

Through the kitchen encounter with Lyndella, Bill had shown us we must provide opportunities for our children to experience many kinds of stimulation. A lemon pie or a glob of cookie dough might provide the necessary stimulation for an otherwise lost mind. We still found that many of our babies died during the first year of their lives. Of those who survive the first two years of life, we found that 16 percent will be able to live without constant supervision, 9 percent become capable of functioning on a level with their peers, and a few are actually unusually brilliant.

Dr. McIntyre, genetic counselor at Case Western

University, Cleveland, was inclined to concur with our belief that hydrocephalic children who have had early corrective surgery show greater potential for extraordinary mental development than the average individual.

Many of our babies would come to have productive lives. Some developed into outstanding young men and women.

Mimi was an example of the life that may lay hidden in any one of those tortured little bodies. At two years of age, she lived in an oxygen tent. She was covered with eczema, her legs were flaccid, and she was unable to communicate. The product of an incestuous relationship, she had been placed with foster parents who were known to be retarded themselves. Mimi's only medical problem was a combination of allergies and deprivation. Through years of patience and tender loving care, the real Mimi was uncovered. She blossomed into a lovely girl and eventually became an accomplished ballet dancer.

Virginia was another case in point. She came to us with a double cleft palate, mylomenongocele, and club feet. Today she is a capable pianist.

Who can say what a deaf child will achieve, or a blind person, a hydrocephalic, or even a retarded baby? I can never forget the possibly brilliant lives that may have been lost for lack of love and proper care.

One day while showing slides to the East Cleveland Rotary Club, a prominent neurosurgeon challenged me for not arranging surgical intervention for all of our hydrocephalic children.

I had no choice but to explain our primary problem to him. Care by most of his fellow physicians cost a great deal of money, and most of our parents and sponsors were something less than wealthy.

God used that meeting, tense as it was, to introduce me to Dr. Clifford Boeckman, pediatrician at Akron Children's

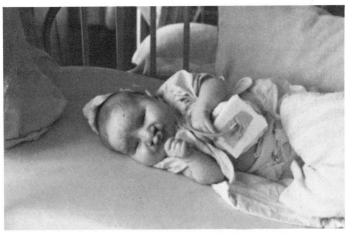

Who can say what a deaf child will achieve, or a blind person, a hydrocephalic, or even a retarded baby? I can never forget the possibly brilliant lives that may have been lost for lack of love and proper care.

Hospital. Dr. Boeckman, a truly compassionate champion of problematic newborns, became the advocate for our children in need of surgery. When he says, "Treat the children early," he means *early*. In his office one day I overheard him speaking to a referring physician from East Liverpool, Ohio.

"Dammit, man, I want these kids immediately!" he shouted into the phone.

"How old was the baby?" I inquired.

"Three hours," he replied. Dr. Boeckman and I understood each other. Thank God for a physician who cares enough to lose his cool. Many children who are healthy today owe their future to this good and dedicated man.

When I heard the story of Johnnie's illness from the lips of his father, my heart was broken. Johnnie had developed acute meningitis following a brief sore throat. On the way to the hospital he stopped breathing. Oxygen administered by the attendant in the ambulance had failed to work. He was pronounced dead on arrival at the emergency room.

His father, however, couldn't accept his death and insisted on resuscitation for his son. After several minutes Johnnie began to breathe again, but was confined to a respirator while physicians fought the vicious meningococci bacteria.

After several weeks he was taken out of the respirator. Three months later the attending physician, Dr. Hostettler, a fine Christian man, who was also a member of our trustee board, told the parents that Johnnie would never regain consciousness and advised them to bring him to the Hattie Larlham Foundation for ongoing care and habilitation.

His grief-stricken parents still believed a miracle would happen. They had faith he would recover. But they were so exhausted that we asked them not to visit for three weeks. We felt they needed time to be alone together and to comfort each other.

Tube-fed, comatose little Johnnie was turned, bathed, massaged, and exercised daily. In a few days his eyes opened; then he began to move about. In time he was up walking, running, and talking.

When his parents dropped in unannounced, he met them as he rode down the corridor on his tricycle. "May we take him to the chapel and thank God?" they asked. I was happy to be able to say yes—for we had carefully designed a chapel into the building.

That night the family dined together for the first time in many months. There was great happiness in the hospital dining room. "May we take him home?" they asked. The answer had to be "no," because his doctor wanted him readmitted to Case Western University Hospital for further brain studies. However, the tests revealed nothing significant in the way of damage. Johnnie was well! In his infinite mercy, God had seen fit to answer intercessory prayer. Johnnie had been touched by the matchless physician.

On Christmas Day, my joy was made complete. His mother called to say, "Johnnie just told us he knew he would be home for Christmas because, when there were no nurses in the room, Jesus came and stood beside his bed and told him so."

Even today when I go into "A" Ward and stand where Jesus stood beside Johnnie that day, I know I am on hallowed ground.

Some through great trial, but God gives a song.

Johnnie's father enrolled in seminary and is now in full-time service for the Lord. Much later when an ambulance screamed up their street one day, Johnnie said to his mother, "That's what I rode in the day I went to be with Jesus, but you wouldn't let me stay."

Have you ever been privileged to speak to someone who has been in heaven? I have. Witnessing to others about the Lord had never been easy for me, but since Johnnie came and went from our Foundation I have had no problem telling others about the power of prayer.

The last chapter of Johnnie's story will be written many years from now, if Jesus tarries, because the message of love continues to work itself out in ways that affect many lives now and even for eternity.

During those years in our little 50-bed facility new programs and new techniques were constantly being developed through our involvement with major medical centers and local universities. Dr. Martha LePow, research scientist from Metropolitan General Hospital, Cleveland, approached Dr. John Allen concerning her work with rubella vaccine. He was, of course, tremendously interested because 20 percent of all major birth defects are the direct result of the measles virus. If a vaccine could be developed to eliminate "three-day measles," we could automatically reduce the numbers of children born to misery. It was a staggering thought.

Dr. Allen brought a proposal to the next meeting of the members of the medical association of the Hattie Larlham Foundation. She suggested developing guidelines for the use of our client population as controls for long-term testing of the effectiveness of the vaccine—after the serum had been proven safe for human use, of course. The proposal was unanimously accepted with great enthusiasm, and we prepared to participate in the research with the full consent of the parents and of our trustee board members.

The development of rubella vaccine is now ancient history, but we were honored to be involved in making medical history. Our small part consisted of the development of long-term studies on effectiveness of the vaccine. For six years Dr. LePow did annual blood tests on the children who had participated, maintaining charts on their continued level of immunity.

We also participated in studies on the new drug "Vallium," for Roche Laboratories. This program was under the direction of Dr. George Sprogus of Hiram University at Hiram, Ohio, a member of our medical association.

We were asked to collaborate with Kent State University's department of psychology in writing a grant application for funding a three-year project on neo-natal cognitive stimulation and developmental training. But that would have to wait. There was not room in our present physical plant.

Dr. Yahner, DDS, applied for staff membership in our organization. He wanted to develop statistics regarding dental problems of the child who was unable to chew. That too must wait. It was becoming obvious that research would play an increasingly important role in our future operation.

No one was more pleased about the direction we were heading than the members of the medical association, especially Dr. Sprogus; research was his first love. It was also becoming apparent that once again something must be done about space.

We had barely learned to walk through the new building without getting lost when we realized we had not built large enough. We needed space—not only for research, but just more space. When the building was erected we had not yet realized how many of our babies might be "salvageable." Our objective had been to plan for as many cribs as possible. Now we were in need of service areas—examining and treatment and therapy rooms, facilities to encourage both physical and cognitive development, laboratories, dentistry, and who could say what else? And, yes, we needed more crib space because once again the list of applications was growing.

Over the holidays, Dick, Lyndella, and I prayed much about what to do and talked constantly of expansion and the directions it might take. Were we going to have outpatient services for homebound preschool children? and how extensive would they be? There were so many things to be considered.

About this time Elmer Stoltzfus made a proposal at one of our board meetings, one that would solve some of our staffing problems, if we decided to expand. He introduced the idea of inviting a Mennonite Voluntary Service unit to assist us. He explained the provision of the United States government whereby conscientious objectors to armed service were permitted to serve their country in other ways. Young men drafted for military training could elect to spend their time in an approved hospital or other essential civilian service. Many Mennonite boys were doing this, and girls too were dedicating a year or two of their lives to a service

A Voluntary Service unit provided a good source of ongoing personnel for our facility.

project. Elmer was convinced that the Hattie Larlham Foundation could qualify as an essential community service. A VS unit, as they are called, should provide a good source of ongoing personnel for our facility, if we could work out a plan for housing the youth.

The board readily took the proposal under advisement and a committee was appointed to work with Elmer toward implementing the program as quickly as possible.

Dick wanted to leave his job and manage the business office; he knew my responsibilities were already too heavy and would become greater if we continued to expand. Already I had difficulty covering all of the fronts adequately. Although he had no clerical training, Dick offered to come into the business office at one third the salary he was presently receiving as an operating engineer. Because my faith was weak, I strongly opposed the move. He had never worked anywhere that paid as well as his present position, I argued. Lyndella was still in college and needed our help. I reminded him that I was receiving little reimbursement for the long hours I put in and we needed his weekly check to keep us afloat. I pointed out that our combined incomes would not be adequate to meet expenses, if he joined our staff. In short, I was totally unwilling for him to make the change.

We talked to various members of the trustee board. Elmer Stoltzfus said, "He who travels alone travels fastest, Dick." Dr. Lang could not understand how an outdoorsman with all the vitality Dick demonstrated could possibly fit himself into the routines of a health facility.

When he felt the time was right, Dick overruled all of us and came to work beside me. From that day forward we worked together, equally committed, but not always as a team. We almost never agreed on strategy. We were still two totally different personalities and my stubborn will made it

111

difficult for me to accept his suggestions. Long ago I had learned to be submissive to my husband, as far as family life was concerned. Ever since he became a Christian he had been the leader in our home. When it came to matters outside the home, where we were equally involved, I stubbornly maintained my right to make decisions.

When Dick came into the business office, his lack of training created problems. Ours was no longer a simplified form of accountability. We needed someone with office management skills to set up and maintain good records. It was determined that we should seek for such a person among our first Voluntary Service applicants, as soon as certification could be obtained for the VS unit.

It was not long until Dick found his niche as director of development, leaving routine business management to those trained in that area. Our roles began to fall into the perspective of many households. He brought in the funds and I spent them. We were beginning to build our organizational chart, without having deliberately planned to do so.

The trustees assumed the task of writing contracts and designating responsibilities. I was formally employed as the administrator and Dick was officially named director of development. Our roles were clearly defined by the language of our contracts.

8
A Solid Institution

The courage of life is often a less dramatic spectacle than the courage of a final moment; but it is no less a magnificent mixture of triumph and tragedy.

John F. Kennedy
Profiles in Courage, 1956

God had given Dick a way with words, great self-confidence, and a zeal for service—an unbeatable combination. His ability to sway an audience left me wondering if in other circumstances he might not have been called to preach the gospel or plead for justice before the bar. From then on I would develop programs, and he would fund them—a fruitful husband-wife relationship.

During the school year Lyndella found jobs on campus to supplement her incomplete tuition funds, and kept up a cheery correspondence with Mom and Dad. When summer vacations came, she accepted her share of responsibility for her fifty small brothers and sisters. She helped with speaking engagements and wrote articles for the news media. We were still a family working together.

Appearing on Easter Straker's live television talk show at Lima, Ohio, Lyndella was asked if she was jealous of our love for all those other children. It was a real blessing to hear her quick response. "It's a funny thing about love, you know. The more you give, the more you have to give." She had learned life's greatest secret early.

With the facility growing more crowded daily, and with the sudden drop in our income, Dick and I accepted a token payment for our home and turned it over to the corporation to be adapted for dormitory use, to accommodate fifteen Mennonite Voluntary Service workers and an advisory couple. We would soon be getting that office manager we needed so badly, and as an extra bonus, a licensed practical nurse. We could certainly use her too. God was rewarding our faithfulness.

We had one of our farm buildings converted into a small cottage and moved into it. Hoping Charles would someday return to finish college, we planned an extra room for him.

Charles did eventually come home to finish his college work at Hiram University but he was not the only one to use that room. Both it and Lyndella's room were eventually occupied by a long series of young people who came to stay with us and work with the children at the hospital.

The first of these was a nurse from Liberia. Our night supervisor had married a young doctor and gone with him to work in Firestone Hospital, Monrovia, Liberia. She wrote to ask if Julia White, the niece of the president of Liberia, could live in our home for a year, work in our hospital, and acquire information pertinent to structuring a department of mental retardation in her country. Here was indeed an open door of opportunity. Of course we would step through it. There had already been a visitor from Italy, seeking factual information, and we had received applications for placement from England, Germany, and Mexico. God was honoring our service.

In due time Julia obtained her passport, visa, and work permit and was on her way to the United States, the country after which Liberia had patterned its government, after the civil war freed Negro slaves to return to their native land.

Having Julia live in our home as a member of the family was an enlightening experience in many ways. She quickly made friends at Kent State University where she sat in classes after her hours on duty at the hospital. It wasn't long until our home was frequented by young people from the African Student Union. Our ears were filled with their plans to return home and become active participants in bringing about the revolutionary movement that would free their country from dominance of the white man. This was not exactly what we had visualized when Julia came to learn about "Child Care and Programming for the Mentally Retarded." Maybe we had not been listening close enough.

Julia was a lovely cultured person, an excellent student,

Julia was the first of many young people who came to learn about infant stimulation while staying in our home.

115

and a good staff nurse. She enrolled at Ball State University in Indiana at the end of her year with us, working on her degree in government and social services before returning to Liberia. We still hear from Julia occasionally. Recently she wrote to say, "You now have a new grandchild called Rabbit Running Up the Hill." Perhaps sometime we will be able to visit Julia in her home. As for the Larlham family, we received a liberal education in world affairs without leaving the confines of our own home.

The compact bungalow on our few remaining acres was easy to care for, and close to the hospital, making it possible for us to spend more time at our chosen occupation. Soon we were at the center twelve and fourteen hours a day, seven days a week, as we took turns being available to talk with parents. This was our big opportunity to witness specifically to the love of Jesus Christ and share the principles of God's Word which never change.

Finally we had to make a decision about expansion—without delay. The expansion this time would take us beyond the realm of homemade blueprints. We would seek federal assistance, enough assistance to hire an architect.

Time was tight, however. Those appropriations for community care centers for the retarded (instigated by the late President John F. Kennedy) had been designated to extend over a four-year period only. They had not yet become available in Ohio for our original building because our state had not yet appropriated matching funds. Now we would apply in the final year. Columbus officials advised us to forget the whole matter. No one believed we would have time to put a grant application together, considering the complex paperwork that the bureaucracy required. However, since it was the only way to expand our facility enough to meet the growing needs of our babies, we certainly had to try.

116

After a conference with state planners, as board member Ned Sargent and I flew back home in his private plane, we made a pact that we would get this money for our children. Ned was not inclined to make large financial contributions himself. His strong forte was leadership, contacts, business expertise, encouragement, and know-how. We would have had a rough time replacing him for those kinds of help.

Grammar had never been my strong subject in school, but I believed that with God's help I could write this grant request, just as his help had enabled me to draw the plans for our first building. Through such experiences faith continues to grow. But help was to come from a source of which we were not aware.

That week I polished off a twelve-page narrative which Dick carefully edited. On Monday we headed for Columbus again. How naive we were. We fell into despair when shown the other detailed applications already submitted—some of them several hundred pages long.

God's arm, however, is not short. He had prepared a man to help with the work of getting that application into shape. A friend from the Bureau of Funding and Grants volunteered to assist us with the application. There couldn't have been a better helper and instructor. The man was kindly but exacting, and he loved his work. He refused to let a single item go unanalyzed. We labored together over that grant request for two weeks, cementing a friendship that would last a lifetime.

By the time all fifteen copies of our 187-page grant application were approved and sent off to Washington, we were just inside the deadline. Much prayer had gone into that stack of paper. My expert helper, a devout Catholic, and I, a humble Protestant, had each stormed the citadels of God in our own ways—he through the apostolate of retarded children and I at prayer meetings with Methodist, Lutheran,

Mennonite, and Baptist friends. Our Jewish board members had also requested their temple priests, under the leadership of Rabbi Rosenthal, to burn incense for our need.

Those were days of difficult decisions and hard labor. While we waited for a response to our grant application, management of the present work continued to demand more and more of my time and energy. Family life consisted of Dick and me working together but rarely seeing each other long enough to discuss anything at all. He was out three or four nights a week raising funds and working long hours developing literature appealing for funds.

Internationally, problems in Vietnam were becoming acute. Six American boys had lost their lives there. It looked as though America would become involved in that Asiatic war. Orpha, when she came over to sew for the children, brought a tape from her son who was serving as a missionary there. In the middle of a sentence about the railroad being built, he interrupted to say, "I must go. Someone has just blown up a bridge." I began to experience fitful nights, tossing as I contemplated the horrors of war and knowing that our two sons were now fully prepared to go overseas if assigned to duty there. Charles had been in skirmishes on the 39th parallel in Korea. Giles, the impetuous one, was an officer in the tank corps. He had a wife and child waiting at home. "Please, God," I prayed, "don't let him go overseas. He will exercise no caution."

The work, the worry, the wear took their toll. My body again began to falter. No matter how good my intentions, physical and emotional exhaustion overtook me. The day came when I literally could not lift my head to voice a need. My strength was not equal to the task; the compound burdens had been too much. But rather than put upon me more than I could bear, God made a way of escape—a forced retreat back to health.

Once again I was carried out of my bed, just as I had been on those two previous occasions. This time our pastor, Robert Balsinger, discovered my plight and took me to the home of Christian friends who providentially had found Christ through their association with our precious babies.

Those friends, JoAnn and Freddie Adsit, urged food down my throat, tended my exhausted body, and prayed, "God, let your will be done in the life of this your servant."

Pains in my abdomen would not go away, and yet I refused to accept the idea of my old enemy, the ulcer, returning. We turned to God's Word and found in 2 Kings 20:1-8 that King Hezekiah had asked for 15 years in which to complete his work.

In the practical realm, we applied ice to my abdomen and heat to my back. The pain left and to this day has not returned.

The night the pain disappeared I was given a vision in my sleep. I saw what our finished physical plant would be like. I saw treatment rooms and equipment that had not yet been conceived. There were developmental cribs which were yet to be designed and produced. God told me in that dream, "This is not for you, but you will see it come to pass."

The disturbing message began to play out in the real world. Insisting on more time to complete the work we had begun, I had forgotten how miserable Hezekiah's final fifteen years were. Likewise, Dick and I were having differences of opinion. Perhaps we had already overstayed our divine mandate, I mused later when things became increasingly difficult. But I was to learn that God was dealing with my husband as never before. When he visited me at my sister Edna's house, where I had gone for three weeks of recuperation, he told me he had sought God diligently in my absence. He was blessed with an infilling of the Holy Spirit unlike anything he had known up to this time.

Troubles would continue their pursuit of us. We are never free of those in this earthly kingdom. But in the meantime, Dick and I set about preparing to build the first addition. Salathiel Barnes, a dear black sister working as a licensed practical nurse, came to us and told how she had received a vision of buildings spreading out across the meadows of our farm. I knew from her description that we had both been privileged to see the same plans. When I laid the sketches from our visions before the board of directors at the next meeting, they were approved for immediate project planning. We were ready to interview architects.

The burst of new activity dictated an addition to our administrative structure. I determined to hire a director of nursing services. We would now have two well-defined departments—a department of development and a department of services. Soon we would need a business manager.

There was never a moment's doubt whom I would select

The completed facility contained 130 cribs with full services.

for our director of nursing services. God had already laid a burden upon my heart that I could no longer ignore.

Since that night long ago when I lay prostrate with lockjaw, there had been a bitterness in my heart for a Christian sister whom I had earlier witnessed to concerning her need for God in her life. Several years had elapsed since my illness without our having resolved what lay between us. Neither she nor I could experience the fullness of God's blessings until the old issue was resolved.

Grace was an excellent pediatric nurse. She had been trained for leadership during her years as a student nurse at University Hospital School of Nursing in Cleveland. I could trust her judgment because I knew of her love for God. Her husband was dying of sarcoma, and she needed work badly to help pay for his treatment. I approached her, we resolved our differences, and she accepted the offer of employment. We never regretted our agreement.

I could rely on Grace to carry out our policies. She and her husband lived nearby, which allowed her to come and go as much as time permitted her to be away from her husband. Grace wrote our manual of procedures and instituted training classes for the nursing aides. It was an excellent arrangement for all of us. And Grace loved our babies. She was God's chosen woman for attending to his special children.

Dick moved vigorously into his expanding public relations assignment, contacting labor unions, the Harness Racers Association of Riders, lodges, industry, individuals, and foundations. Directing the development of funding resources was no longer only a matter of speaking at churches and women's groups, although that was still important. The operation of his department became highly sophisticated as staff grew and outreach expanded. Our list of individual donors included thousands of names. Added to this were the foundations and organizations. All required follow-up and gracious recognition. No longer could Edna do this on the few hours a week she could spend at the foundation. We no longer spoke of "fund raising" per se. Public relations was an integral part of the process. Through God's grace, my wonderful Christian husband had the insight and sensitivity to design literature, formulate letters, and make contacts that kept funds coming in to support the work as it grew. He had found his work for God in our combined place of service. He was now raising tens of thousands of dollars a year to meet operating expenses.

Through all of this my sisters, of necessity, became more personally involved in the women's auxiliary but retained their interest in the hospital. As Dick's responsibilities increased, theirs decreased. This was difficult for them. But the sisters retained their interest in the foundation, continuing to promote various fund-raising and service projects through the women's auxiliary programs. Flea markets, rummage sales, Christmas bazaars, musicals, bake sales, and dozens of other hard labor projects—all highly productive—were successful because of their organization and leadership.

The expansion program we were to undertake would lead us into a strange new world in other ways, as well as fund raising. We would no longer be scrambling to make space for new cribs alone. We now knew that a crib did not provide everything the baby would need. We had caught a new vision of the importance of habilitation. Play and stimulation was of the utmost importance at the earliest moment possible, and such facilities would take much more than a crib's worth of space. In this expansion we would need to allow room for bedside supportive equipment, therapy rooms, dental services. Our new programs would be unusually comprehensive, certainly an ambitious goal. Building for the future, some parts of the building would be left open for yet undesignated programs to be conducted by experts in many disciplines. And, yes, we would provide for outpatient diagnostic and treatment services.

How much space and what kind of equipment would our home trainers need for parents of the homebound? Who would use our clinic and/or the day care facilities? How many children and workers would be able to occupy each area comfortably at a given time? There were no guidelines; we had nowhere to go for assistance or information; we were breaking new ground. How long would it be before other facilities like ours would be developed? We hoped it would not be many years before others profited by our experience and our errors in judgment.

With God's leadership, we built our physical plant around planned program—a program that was years in advance of any similar thinking of which we were aware. We were designing a laboratory in which God would produce his miracles.

Just as we had been led to the right people in the financial world, we were now making the necessary contacts in the scientific arena. We became acquainted with professionals who had skills and know-how we had never imagined. I still find it amazing that God allowed us to be the catalyst to bring it all together.

God leads his dear children along.

Truly this mission field had no limits. Never were the harvest fields more challenging. Even as our faces became well known through the power of the news media, we knew we had nothing to fear from anyone, because God had prepared the way. "If God be for us, who can be against us?" (Romans 8:31). He had built a fence around us (Job 10:11), and we found the Word of God to be as effective with intellectual giants as it was with desperate parents. God is no respecter of persons.

An example of God's guiding hand can be found in the chapel nestled within the walls of our new wing at the hospital. Planning this chapel in the expanded area became a major challenge. The trustees could not reconcile themselves to spending money for a place of worship, since the cost could not be included in our grant application. The very people on the trustee board whose hearts had grown tender through exposure to our babies were resistant to spending money exclusively for a place of worshiping and glorifying God. Friction arose as to whether or not we could risk preparing a worship center for Gentiles when we were intimately involved with many people of Jewish faith. Sheldon Epstein, calling our attention to the prominent luminous cross on the front of the building, asked if we would place the Star of David in the proposed chapel. I reminded him we were all worshiping one Lord and God, the Creator of all mankind.

The prayer and faith chapter of the women's auxiliary, under Winnie's guidance, laid this problem before the throne of grace with prayer and fasting. Then the Hartville Mennonite ladies suggested selling hot home-baked pies in downtown Ravenna to raise money for building the chapel. A rummage sale was planned in conjunction with the pie sale. It was so successful that the sale lasted three full days. Pies were loaded into stationwagons filled with racks for the trips between Hartville and Ravenna. Our East Cleveland chapter, with their mercantile connections, worked out fantastic bargains in clothing, which were labeled "nearly-nice." A mink stole donated by one of the Jewish parents brought $800 toward our chapel project.

Soon the chapel had become a reality of loveliness, beautifully furnished with hand-carved furniture, velvet drapes, a deep carpet, subdued light, and a stained-glass window containing the Rose of Sharon motif. It was designed and wrought by a famous artisan from Italy. This lovely little nook in our busy service institution has been a great source of comfort to both families and staff, whether Jew or Gentile, Catholic or Protestant. The chapel is our visible evidence of esteem for the Provider of all good things.

With completion of the expansion project, a new area of service opened before us. As the work grew, Dick and I were becoming further removed from the intimacy of direct service. By now our administrative structure was well developed and I could allocate most of the decision-making to department directors. At an age when most women are enjoying their grandchildren I had entered an educational program to prepare me for licensing as a nursing home administrator, a title soon to be required in our increasingly sophisticated operation. I no longer had direct contact with parents and staff. Most of all, I missed the children. They were still there,

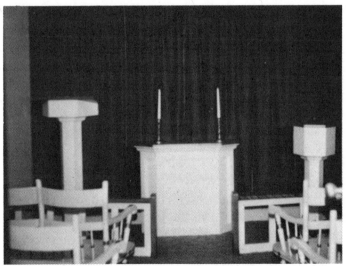

The chapel in our busy service institution has been a source of comfort to both families and staff, whether Jew or Gentile, Catholic or Protestant.

but in a sense I was not. I was learning that the high pinnacles are lonely places.

The children no longer knew me well enough to yearn for my presence when I left the room, except Sylvia—she would always be my own. Many evenings I spent beside her crib after long days in the office. The affections of the others were given to the attendants who rocked and sang to them, changed their diapers, and helped them learn to grasp their first toy.

Both Dick and I were feeling the absence of that special quality in our lives that comes from the closeness of human relationship. Our hearts were yearning toward our own offspring who by now had returned from their faraway places, married, and started their own families.

It seemed that even Dick and I rarely had time together. Although we were sharing the same achievements, our paths were widely divergent. I was tied to my administrative desk and he to his fund-raising office. When we had time together, there was little to talk about except our individual problems. Just as our own children had grown up and developed their own life patterns, so had this work come to maturity. It was a highly sophisticated institution offering skilled medical services, therapeutic care, training, and education—and operating on a million-dollar budget. Time to move on? No, not yet.

I could write of planning the next expansion, completing the design in the vision God had given me, but to what point? It was similar to previous advances in design and program development. After architectural design was completed and approved for the maximum number of individuals permitted in a private residential facility, we began imploring God to provide the means for our retirement.

We decided to approach the executive committee of the trustee board with our problem. We found they had already been discussing the matter among themselves, not quite knowing how to tell us that we should be looking for someone to take over management when we retired. After lengthy deliberation they suggested that we try to find a Christian group who would agree to provide ongoing administration, assuring continuity and preserving the philosophy of the founders.

When approached, the Catholic diocese quickly declined, overtaxed with too many charities at that time. Sheldon and Avery asked that we concentrate on Protestant church bodies. So we formulated a letter stating our need and requesting an early response from four major groups: Methodist, Lutheran, United Church of Christ, and Mennonite denominations. Of those four, only the United Church of Christ and the Mennonite Church responded with proposals.

Each proposal had merit. Our long association with Mennonite individuals swung the balance in that direction and the vote was cast in their favor.

The fifteen years I had committed to complete the work were rapidly drawing to a close. We had been faithful. We could trust God to watch over us down through the waning years of life. We began to sing the hymn that Lyndella would use as her solo contribution at our retirement dinner in the near future.

> Under his wings, I am safely abiding . . .
>
> Under his wings, O what precious enjoyment!
> There will I hide till life's trials are o'er;
> Sheltered, protected, no evil can harm me;
> Resting in Jesus I'm safe evermore.
>
> Under his wings, under his wings,
> Who from his love can sever?
> Under his wings my soul shall abide,
> Safely abide forever. . . .

We had assurance those coming years might be the most wonderful of our entire life. God would provide someone with more administrative training than I who could handle the technical details with greater skill.

Our trustee board, with great foresight, entered into an assumption agreement with the Mennonite Board of Missions of the Mennonite Church, wherein they committed themselves to provide continuous and ongoing qualified Christian administration of the Hattie Larlham Foundation after retirement of the present administration. They also wrote into the agreement assurance that the present philosophy and purpose would be maintained by the board of trustees, as outlined in the present code of regulations.

It then became the responsibility of the Mennonite Board of Missions, through its Health and Welfare Department, to submit for our consideration and the trustee board's ultimate

Esther and Isaac Alderfer, Mennonite VS leaders for us.

approval the names of various qualified individuals for the post of director. Participating in the selection and then working with the person of choice, Paul Kurtz, PhD, for a three-month transition period, brought me to the realization of how my sisters had felt as they lessened their activities at the foundation. The day of retirement was now fully upon us in so far as our work at the foundation was concerned, but I was not yet ready to leave the field of private residential care for the mentally retarded and developmentally disabled.

Following our retirement dinner, where Fred Krouse, executive secretary of the President's Committee on Mental Retardation, presented me with a lifetime honorary membership on the committee, I admitted to myself that I could not abruptly break away from the long habit of daily concentrated involvement and concern with the affairs of the mentally retarded. I was too much concerned about the rapid growth of private residential care facilities in local communities. Too much had happened too fast. The federal mandate to deinstitutionalize had emptied our state institutions into the communities before there had been time to prepare for them. There were lack of programs, lack of trained operators, lack of community acceptance. In short, there was great danger of these homes becoming even more ineffectual than our previous system of state warehouses.

Several years previously, when the exodus first began, those of us who were concerned had taken time from our busy schedules to organize the National Association of Private Residential Facilities for the Mentally Retarded (NAPRFMR), with headquarters in Washington, D.C. The 54-member board of trustees of this nonprofit corporation consisted of private residential operators who represented individual states and regions throughout the nation. It was the responsibility of the state representatives on that board to monitor legislative action pertaining to the mentally retarded in that state, and to strive for the development of a viable chapter in each state that would, in some degree, provide self-regulation of our numerous private facilities.

My final quest, then, would be the organization of private operators in Ohio to give us the political clout we needed in Columbus. It was time for me to move to our capital city.

It was November of 1978 when we left the foundation. Great strides had been made in the seventeen years we had spent creating services for profoundly dysfunctional newborn infants and preschool children, and in working with others to bring a better way of life for all retarded persons.

Dick moved to the western part of Ohio to be near our daughter and her family. Our greatest anticipation was to share the remainder of our lives with our eight grand-children—four girls and four boys, ranging from 13-year-old Michael to one-year-old Jamie and Elizabeth. It had been so long since we had time to spend with our own children that we could hardly wait. Nevertheless, that first year I found it necessary to divide my time between the community where we would eventually live and the apartment-office combination I had rented in Columbus. At sixty-four I had undertaken another monumental work.

The Ohio Private Residential Association, Inc., (OPRA), began by prayer and faith, just as The Hattie Larlham Foundation, Inc., had several years before, except that this time I was in a hurry. There was an even bigger difference too. By now there was a bit more *savoir-faire*. Years of experience in dealing with officials in Columbus and working through the political system had developed the necessary know-how to expedite what was to be done. God's training classes had prepared me well.

In just one year the organization was completed and the association had located and employed a qualified executive secretary. More than 60 percent of the operators of private facilities in Ohio had joined OPRA, which meant the organization would have a strong voice in establishing policy for care of the retarded in Ohio. But how that entire action came about is certainly not part of this narrative.

Suffice it to say, I was now at last satisfied to retire—totally and completely ready. The Hattie Larlham Foundation was under good supervision and the work for the rights of the retarded will go on. The structure for continuity had been established. God's precious children will be cared for more adequately because the vision has been expanded.

Dick and I with our own children and their families.

Dick and I thank God for permitting us to have a small part in the advancement of so great a service to mankind.

It has been an intensely personal challenge for our family—not only Dick and I, but our children as well. Our son Giles and his wife, Kathy, lost four of the eight children she delivered, while we were providing shelter and comfort for others. Three of our own grandchildren died during the first 10 days of life because of anomalies. It was after the third baby that Giles turned his life over to God, left his position at Seiberling Rubber and went to Bible seminary in Missouri.

As the shadows of evening gather, we face the sunset of life with our remaining grandchildren and children around us. What could be better? Inept and unworthy as we have been, we are grateful that God has accepted us also as his own dear children.

Under his wing I am safely abiding....

Since retirement, Dick and I have been privileged to do some of the things we both dreamed of. He loves to travel. It is my joy to combine travel with volunteer work for God.

Soon after I left the Columbus office, Dick began talking about taking me to Venezuela. I wanted to see Latin America, but was more interested in going to Central America because there were two young men in Guatemala in whom we had an interest. They were Myan Indian fellows whom we had sponsored in the mission school at Quiche. Elmer Alverado had graduated from school as an accountant and was now working with Children's Services International, helping find Christian homes for displaced children. Diago Raymundo Marcos would soon finish high school and had expressed a desire to become a medical doctor. How nice it would be to become better acquainted with these two foster children from a different culture!

Diago Marcos, a Mayan Indian in Guatemala, whom we
sponsored in the mission school at Quiche.

It had been only three years since the devastating earth-
quake in Guatemala. The mission board accepted us as
volunteers, not laden with responsibilities, but free to choose
when and where we would assist. Michael, our oldest grandchild, went with us. What a joy! We bought a VW Camp-
mobile and set out to spend six months in Guatemala, the
land of eternal spring. It was a marvelous experience for
Mike, and we did get to know Diago and agreed to continue
our sponsorship while he went to college. We were delighted
to find that both young men are totally dedicated to God.
Diago wants to go back to his native tribe, carrying the good

news of salvation and bringing health services where there have been none.

I had learned something of the needs of the people in outlying villages in the Sierra Madras. Part of my volunteer work consisted of flying with the bush pilots to inaccessible areas to bring medical services. Often the tribespeople

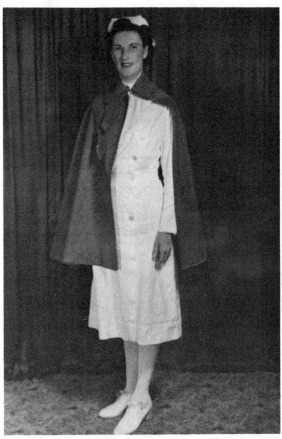

The mountain girl from West Virginia has come "a fur piece," but not beyond the shadow of her father's early training.

would only see the plane twice a year. Otherwise, they depended on witch doctors, whom they feared and hated but consulted of necessity. They had not yet heard of the love of God. We thank God because he has given us the opportunity to assist in preparing these two fine Christian men in another part of our world to serve him and bring the wonderful message of salvation to others.

More recently, we spent a winter at Teen Missions International headquarters on Merritt Island in Florida. Dick was especially happy to work at public relations again. They were preparing and mailing out literature inviting teenagers to commit a summer of their lives to spreading the gospel in Third World countries.

We have the assurance of good things to follow in our remaining retirement years, as long as we keep our part of the covenant we have made with God.

The little mountain girl from West Virginia and her beloved husband have come "a fur piece," but not beyond that long shadow of her father's early training.

God leads his dear children along.

Appendix 1

Retirement Address

Family, parents—former residents, co-workers, media, honorable officials, all friends of God's precious children, thank you for your presence here tonight. For Dick and me this is a humbling and rewarding climax to several years of happiness experienced in hard work. For each of us, there is a place God would have us stand. We are filled with humility, having been allowed to serve the retarded in Ohio during the years of rapidly changing concepts. This has been a thrilling and rewarding experience (1) because of the truly great officials and other friends of the retarded we have worked with, (2) because of the tremendous strides that have been made toward more humanized care and treatment, and (3) because of the beginning of community awareness of what the needs and responses are, and how they may be met more effectively.

Any part we may have had in helping to achieve the present

Given by Hattie Larlham at an appreciation dinner held at Kent State University Student Center Ballroom on Sunday, September 18, 1977, at the time of her retirement.

level of programming, either here at the Hattie Larlham Foundation or elsewhere, has been made possible because of the Holy Spirit working through us to perform the will of God in our lives and the lives of those whom he loves most—our children.

James tells us, "God has chosen the poor to be heirs of the kingdom." Your spiritual leader may speak to you of spiritual poverty, or lack of earthly goods. I speak of another kind of poverty—our physically and mentally impoverished children here in the foundation are of all people most impoverished—they are sure to become heirs of God's marvelous kingdom. We are most privileged to have had the opportunity of serving them in some small measure.

It seems fitting that the initials of our name "H - L - F" stands for "Hope - Love - Faith." It is more fitting to read from the right, as our Oriental friends do:

Faith is the foundation on which this present work was built. Because of that strong foundation, a superstructure can now be laid.

Love has been the key to works made perfect through faith. Seventeen years of a committed service requires mental and emotional preparation for retirement. The human ego thrives on status; we cling to it tenaciously. However, time is fleeting and this pain shall pass, too. Knowing the quality of our successor makes leaving less difficult. Knowing the dedication of those staying with Dr. Paul Kurtz is reassuring. Knowing the quality of state officials who are the "watchdogs" of good programming gives us reason to hope.

Hope continues springing eternal in the breast of man. We know that "he who began this good work" will not let it die simply because Dick and I have completed our assignment here. A new person has been called to continue what has been started here. In the beginning, God promised us fifteen years. They have been great years. He also promised friends to be our hands. To each of you who have been those hands—helping fulfill our vision—I now say, Stand beside Dr. Kurtz as faithfully as you have stood with Dick and me. He will need your prayers, your dollars, and your talents to build the new structure and to develop the planned programs.

Please pray for Dick and me, as we hand this policy manual to our successor, that we may have peace in our twilight years. Pray for Dr. Kurtz, that he may always believe in *"the value of life itself, regardless of apparent lack of achievement potential in the given individual."*

We love each of you and commend you for your faithful service to God's special heirs to his kingdom.

It is my prayer that you will accept that responsibility as one of the human race, that you will submit yourself wholly to the Lord God, giving your heart and soul to the work at hand.

Dick and I at the Kent State appreciation dinner.

Declaration of Rights

This declaration of rights of a person who is mentally retarded or otherwise developmentally disabled is prepared with the full knowledge that we are:

1. MINDFUL of the pledge of the United Nations to take joint and separate action to promote higher standards of living, full employment, and improved conditions of economic progress and development.

2. REAFFIRMING faith in human rights and fundamental freedoms, in the principles of peace, dignity, and worth of the human person and in the full understanding of social justice.

3. RECALLING principles developed and enunciated by national and international organizations which collectively state principles developing all aspects of the rights of the human being.

4. EMPHASIZING that this document builds upon others in proclaiming the necessity of protecting the rights and assuring the welfare and rehabilitation of physically and mentally disadvantaged, of mentally retarded and developmentally disabled.

5. BEARING IN MIND the need to assist each person to develop his abilities to the utmost and of promoting as far as possible his appropriate placement in the continuum of life patterns.

We proclaim, therefore, this Declaration of Rights of a Person Who Is Mentally Retarded or Otherwise Developmentally Disabled and we do call for individuals and organizations on the local, national, or international scene to support the common basic fundamentals of this statement and to develop an attitude for the provision and the protection of these rights.

The person who is mentally retarded or otherwise developmentally disabled:

1. Has the same rights as other human beings, and those rights should be provided and protected to the maximum degree.

2. Has the right to proper medical care, therapy and treatment, education, training, rehabilitation and guidance and to such other modalities as will enable him to develop his maximum ability, potential, and obtain the greatest level of achievement.

3. Has the right of economic security and decent standard of living.

4. Has the right to perform appropriate productive work or engage in other meaningful occupation to the extent of his capabilities.

5. Has the right to live in a social situation which will provide the greatest opportunities for his own development for improving socialization with family, community, and friends which is best suited for his immediate and overall needs and which is provided in surroundings and circumstances as appropriate and consistent with his individual or multiple developmental problems.

6. Has the right to qualified and responsible guardianship if such is necessary to protect his well being and his interests.

7. Has the right to protection from exploitation, abuse, and degrading treatment of any kind and a right to due process of law with full recognition to his needs and to the requirements of others with whom he may be involved.

8. Has the right to exercise his rights in a meaningful fashion and to be provided safeguards through legal and human channels, through due process, through professional guidance to prevent any form of abuse.

9. Has the right to professional services for habilitation, training, care, education as determined by competent professionals with such evaluations, determinations, and programming subject to appropriate review and the right of appeal to higher professional and/or legal authorities.

The Hattie Larlham Foundation subscribes to the above statement of rights as developed by the National Association of Private Residential Facilities for the Mentally Retarded. Reprinted by permission.

Born Hattie Lena Gadd, Mrs. Larlham grew up at Reader, West Virginia. She graduated from the Youngstown (Ohio) Hospital Association School of Nursing, did continuing education at Kent State University, and received her license as a nursing home administrator after completing a course of study from George Washington University.

Mrs. Larlham is cofounder of The Hattie Larlham Foundation, Inc. (a model residential care center for profoundly handicapped infants) and served as its administrator from 1961 to 1977.

She was inducted into the Ohio Hall of Fame by Governor

James Rhodes in 1980 for her contribution to the care of handicapped infants. In 1977 she was named as a special adviser to the President's Committee on Mental Retardation. Rosalyn Carter said, "Your selfless dedication and devotion to providing care for so many handicapped young children deserves unique recognition, for these children are indeed among the most vulnerable in our society. I believe our success as a nation must be measured by the compassion we show the most vulnerable among us."

Mrs. Larlham founded the Ohio Private Residential Association in 1974 and served as its executive secretary until 1979. She is a member of the American Nurses' Association and has worked with the Ohio Association for Retarded Citizens, the American Association for Mental Deficiency, and the National Association of Private Residential Facilities for Mentally Retarded.

She speaks to women's, civic, and church organizations, and is available as a consultant wherever her services are required.

She lives with her husband, Richard R. Larlham, in retirement at St. Mary's, Ohio. They are the parents of three adult children, Richard, Giles, and Lyndella. Hattie and Richard are members of the Frost Road Primitive Methodist Chapel at Streetsboro, Ohio, and currently attend the Christian Union Church at Buckland.

God Leads Us Along

G. A. Y.

G. A. YOUNG

1. In shad-y green pas-tures so rich and so sweet, God leads His dear
2. Some-times on the mount where the sun shines so bright, God leads His dear
3. Tho' sor-rows be-fall us and Sa-tan op-pose, God leads His dear
4. A-way from the mire, and a-way from the clay, God leads His dear

chil-dren a-long. Where the wa-ter's cool flow bathes the wea-ry one's feet,
chil-dren a-long. Some-times in the val-ley in the dark-est of night,
chil-dren a-long. Through grace we can con-quer, de-feat all our foes.
chil-dren a-long. A-way up in glo-ry, e-ter-ni-ty's day,

CHORUS

God leads His dear children a-long. Some thro' the waters, some thro' the flood

Some thro' the fire, but all thro' the Blood; Some thro' great sor-row, but

rit.

God gives a song In the night sea-son and all the day long.